THE
GAY MAN'S
KAMA
SUTRA

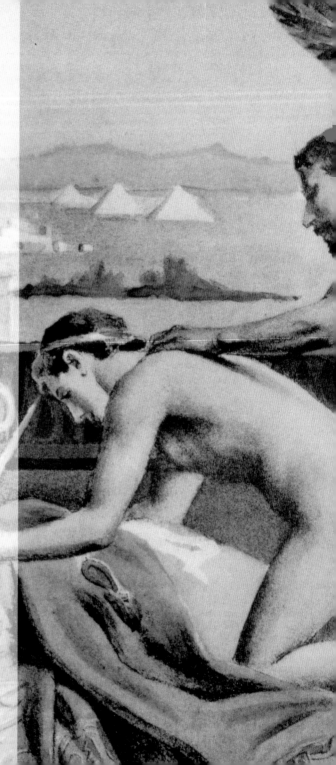

THIS IS A CARLTON BOOK

Text copyright ©2003 Terry Sanderson
Design copyright ©2003 Carlton Books
Limited

This edition first published in 2010
by Carlton Books Limited
20 Mortimer Street
London W1T 3JW

Reprinted in 2011, 2015

10 9 8 7 6 5 4 3

ISBN 978 1 84732 714 7

Printed and bound in Hong Kong

Editorial Manager: Judith More
Editorial and Design: Axis Design
Production Controller: Kate Pimm
Picture Researcher: Elena Goodinson
Illustrator: Roger Payne
Index: Indexing Specialists

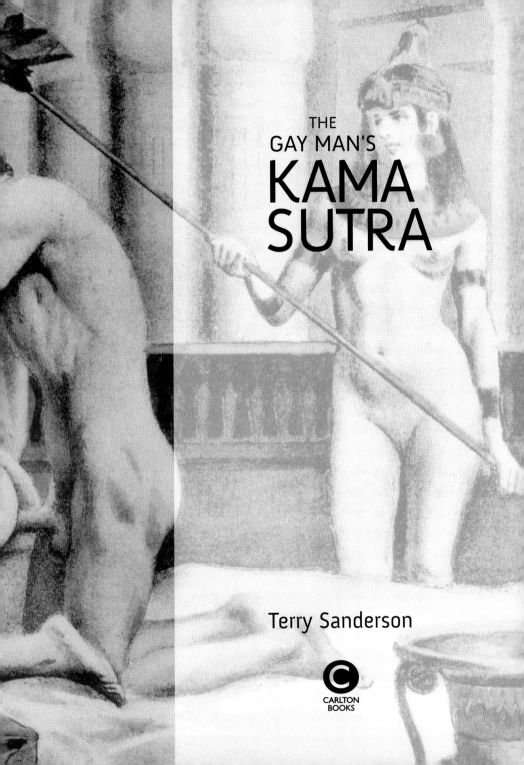

THE
GAY MAN'S
KAMA
SUTRA

Terry Sanderson

CARLTON
BOOKS

contents

introduction

history

Almost 2,500 years ago, an Indian
scholar of the Brahmin caste named
Vatsyayana distilled a collection of
ancient texts on sex and good living into
a book called the *Kama Sutra*, aimed at
educating young people in the ways of
love as practised in their culture.

ABOVE Sex is a fundamental human impulse that will not be denied. All attempts to control and regulate it have ultimately failed. Love knows no locksmith.

OPPOSITE Same sex love has been present throughout recorded history. Sometimes it has been validated and enjoyed; often, it has been violently persecuted.

Vatsyayana's work was not translated into English until 1883.
The translators, Sir Richard Burton and F. F. Arbuthnot, believing
that it would generate huge controversy in Victorian society,
published it anonymously.

The *Kama Sutra* did not become generally available to the public
in England until the 'permissive age' of the 1960s. The book's fame
spread rapidly after that, and it soon became part of the consciousness
of Western culture. It has achieved iconic status on its reputation
alone and there are few who are unaware of the existence of the *Kama
Sutra*, though many people may never have seen a copy.

But the *Kama Sutra* is far more than a book about acrobatic
sex. It is a manual for living. It is probably one of the first 'how-
to', self-help books ever written, and seeks to cover the whole
gamut of thought about how men and women should relate to each
other in order to create an orderly and civilized society.

While the *Kama Sutra* advocates the uninhibited enjoyment of the pleasures of the flesh, it also counsels that those pleasures be used for a higher purpose. Sex and sensual indulgence are not to be despised, but they should simply be part of our striving for understanding of man's place not only in the world, but also in this fleeting moment in eternity that we all inhabit.

The *Kama Sutra* was originally written in the ancient Indian language of Sanskrit, and roughly translates as 'The Rules of Love' – *kama* means 'love, pleasure and sensuality' and *sutra* means 'aphorism', the expression of an idea in as few words as possible.

Vatsyayana considered the book to have a religious dimension. He said he had written it 'according to the precepts of Holy Writ' and that it had a nobler purpose than just the promotion of pleasure. Read carefully, the *Kama Sutra* is, indeed, a manual for the good citizen of its day.

The resurgence of interest in ancient Eastern philosophies, as well as medicines and therapies, has given the *Kama Sutra* a new relevance. Its philosophy of sex chimes more realistically with the experience and expectation of a modern, well-educated and affluent population than do those of Western religions.

In this book, I have adapted the spirit of the *Kama Sutra* to fit the mores and needs of modern gay men. For, although the many sexual positions described in the *Kama Sutra* are intended for the delectation of men and women, they don't need much modification to be used by two men.

The urge to seek and obtain sexual gratification is timeless. It is a fundamental drive in nearly all living creatures. The *Kama Sutra* accepts that truth as self-evident, and its whole philosophy springs from it. Our sexual impulses are seen as good and worthy; when it

ABOVE Despite social disapproval and criminal sanctions, gay men have always managed to find each other and express their affection in the way that is right for them.

was written, those impulses had not yet been overlaid with the anti-sex proscriptions that have become so common in mono-theistic religions throughout the world.

However, unlike sex urges, the rules of societies are far from timeless – they can, and do, change. Laws and taboos vary from one generation to another and from one civilization to the next.

In the two and a half millennia that have passed since the *Kama Sutra* was created, civilizations have come and gone, religions have lived and died, and what seemed like eternal decrees have been discarded and replaced. Societies see the world as it is reflected in their own environment and their own time; no two reflections are alike. The urge for sexual fulfilment, however, is constant, unchanging and fundamental to us all.

Because of this, we have to consider the society in which the *Kama Sutra* originated. It was very different from the one we inhabit almost 2,500 years later. We cannot pretend that centuries of human endeavour and scientific progress have not brought knowledge that can be added to the treasure trove of the *Kama Sutra*.

The world into which the *Kama Sutra* was born was, in many ways, cruel and elitist. The caste system condemned the majority to a lifetime of extreme poverty, drudgery and early death. Meanwhile, a few at the top of the system lived in luxury, spending their days in idle amusement and indulgence.

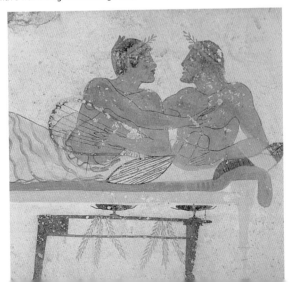

BELOW In ancient Greece, an institutionalized form of homosexuality involved an older man 'mentoring' a younger man by instructing him in the ways of good citizenship.

In the modern Western world, with its affluence, egalitarianism and concern for human rights, most of us can now enjoy what the Brahmin caste alone enjoyed in the days of Vatsyayana.

The main aim of the *Kama Sutra*, then, is to acquire knowledge and power through virtue, prosperity and love. With a little luck, and a lot of effort, we can experience all three. We are wealthy enough to be able to explore and pamper our senses; we have education as a right; and enough leisure time to indulge our desires if we so wish.

So, in the light of accumulated knowledge, we need to take from the *Kama Sutra* that which is relevant to our lives today. We can identify what is timeless and discard that which is temporary and culture bound. We would not want to embrace some of the philosophy, particularly that which asserts that the vast majority of the human race are to be regarded as nothing more than servants and vassals because of their lowly birth, or that some of them are even 'untouchable'.

Indian society – then as now – is complex, and the same culture that produced the sex-affirming *Kama Sutra* also produced philosophies of extreme prudery that even today forbids Bollywood actors to kiss on screen.

So, we take that which is anchored in the human condition – the urge for love, sex and sensual indulgence – and we discard that which has passed into history – the prejudices of a society that was of another place and another time.

We must be honest and recognize that the *Kama Sutra* is ambiguous about gay sex, regarding it as the province of eunuchs and effeminates. It equates male–male love exclusively with fellatio, which is condemned because it is primarily practised by male prostitutes. Oral sex is referred to as Superior Coition, because the entry of the *lingam* (penis) takes place at a point higher up the body than in genital–genital intercourse. Although the *Kama Sutra* reluctantly concedes that fellatio is also practised 'in the best society', it is, nevertheless, denounced as 'indecent, anti-social and uncivilized'.

Vatsyayana includes a whole chapter on the practice of fellatio, in which eunuchs are referred to as the 'third sex'.

He may have been describing the Hijras, a religious sect that is still to be found in modern India. This all-male group, whose present-day numbers are estimated at between fifty and five-hundred thousand, divide themselves into two classes: those who surgically remove their penis and those who remain intact. The sect worships the Mother Goddess and seeks to identify with her by becoming as feminine as possible.

Their traditional role in Northern India is that of entertainers. Although they purport to uphold the ideal of chastity, many Hijras act as prostitutes, taking the passive role for Indian men who regard them merely as convenient substitutes for women. In this way these men can reassure themselves that their sexual identity is still unquestionably heterosexual.

ABOVE The Hijras' acceptance of sexual ambiguity has provided a haven for many gay people from a culture that frequently uses marriage as a means of social advancement.

ABOVE In the wake of severe proscriptions in their own society, Victorian artists used an imaginary classical culture as an excuse to explore erotic themes.

In her study of the Hijras, Serena Nadra says that many teenage homosexuals who are rejected by their families find their way into Hijra circles. There they discover acceptance in a kind of niche, protecting them from a society that rejects any mode of living outside the traditional family structure. Although there is disagreement about the extent to which Indian society tolerates the Hijras, they do provide some kind of legitimacy and social status for homosexuals, transvestites and transsexuals.

The only other way for Indian homosexual men to escape the unrelenting pressure to marry has been for them to leave their family, renounce their caste and take up the unattached life of a monk, guru, teacher or wandering holy man. It is easy to see that many men who could not countenance even a sham heterosexual life for themselves would follow that path and, in so doing, find themselves in the company of other men of like mind.

So, although India – ancient and modern – may be in denial about homosexuality, it has always existed and has been practised covertly. The earliest surviving text on Indian law is the *Arthashastra* from the fourth century BCE. Its author, Kautilya, prescribes fines of 48 to 94 *pana*s for male homosexual activity, and 12 to 24 *panas* for lesbianism. These fines were much lower than for heterosexual offences.

The best known of the Indian sacred law texts is the *Code of Manu*, which dates from the first to the third centuries CE. This prescribes that an upper-class man who 'commits an unnatural act with a male...shall bathe, dressed in his clothes'. An expiation ritual is also ordered for any man who swallows semen. The members of the lowest four castes, as well as outcastes, suffered no restrictions as they weren't considered important enough to fall within the ambit of the law.

So, homosexuality has always been prevalent in India, although it has not been celebrated in quite the same way as heterosexual love. But while this male-dominated society might permit men to be the aggressor in a sexual encounter with another man, being the passive partner was taboo. A special kind of contempt was, and is, reserved for men who allow themselves to be penetrated. Eventually, Christianity and more intolerant forms of Hinduism and Islam held sway. Then, the celebration of sex that had been the norm in the days of Vatsyayana gave way to prurience and disapproval.

From this rich cultural hotch-potch, we will draw out the best advice for the ways of love and how to apply them to our own lives in the twenty-first century. We will strip away the guilt and shame with which the instructions in the *Kama Sutra* have become associated in succeeding centuries, and embrace the joy and ecstasy that is truly human.

Chapter 1:
On being gay

the art of male love

In the *Kama Sutra*, the practice and perfection of the techniques of love were to be accompanied by other accomplishments that were held to be of equal value.

A man must strive to become a learned poet, someone who can appreciate beauty in its many manifestations. He should decorate and perfume his home and his body with rich ornamentation and fragrance. He should appreciate the timelessness and beauty of music and be able to express his love through singing and the playing of an instrument.

He should be able to comport himself well in any company, and be skilled in the subtle art of conversation and language. He will also use flowers and plants of great beauty to create aesthetic pleasure in his everyday environment. He will throw the most delicate of these flowers at his lover as a token of his pleasure and as a signal of his intentions.

He will surround himself with fine art and objects that have been created by loving hands.

He will cultivate all that is good and pleasing to the senses. Mountains and streams, trees and animals – all the natural world will be regarded with respect. He will consider himself to be an integral part of that world and will be at one with his fellow creatures.

Love cannot be separated from other aspects of life, and a life devoted to the best and most worthy pursuits will eventually translate into noble and fulfilling sex. The more that we know of the arts and sciences, the more we will come to know about ourselves. A man who is cultured and knowledgeable, not only about academic subjects, but also about matters of human nature, will be better equipped to enjoy supreme love.

ABOVE The idealized images of mythology inspired European artists to depict the kind of intimacy, and nudity, that they could not otherwise portray.

With this in mind, the *Kama Sutra* advises men to:

- study music
- study dance and movement
- know the stars and planets and the heavenly bodies
- gain knowledge of dictionaries and vocabularies
- practise handwriting so that notes and letters can be sent to the beloved
- master the art of drawing, and learn tattooing, which is an extension of drawing
- study architecture and the art of house building
- study interior design, arranging couches, beds and cushions in pleasing ways and lighting these areas with subtlety
- make money honestly and be just in dealing with others
- cook well, creating appetizing dishes
- master the art of using spices, not only to flavour dishes, but to perfume the air and the body with intense aromatics that seduce the beloved
- explore the use of perfumes and unguents as a means of massaging the flesh of the beloved
- exercise in the gymnasium so that his body will be pleasing to look at and able to move with grace, and manoeuvre in ways that will please his lover
- enjoy the art of gardening, and thereby become close to nature
- become fluent in languages so that he can be at home in many countries – always respecting cultures whose norms and rules may not match his own
- treat others with respect and charity
- be aware of body language, including how to understand gestures and expressions

LEFT The satyr is teaching the youth to play the pipes. In the formalized homosexuality of Greek society, the life skills that older men – as mentors – passed on to the next generation included the skills of lovemaking.

- be informed about, and skilled in the use of, all means of effective communication
- be skilled in all kinds of sports and games
- have knowledge of the art of diplomacy
- be skilled in the use of technology of all kinds
- be able to care for the sick, and to tend animals with the same reverence as humans.

If a man can master at least some of these skills (ten is the optimum number) and if he has a pleasant disposition, beauty and other winning qualities, then his place in the world as a respected citizen will be guaranteed. He will never want for suitors to beg for his favours, and he could have a new lover every night if he wanted. But he would know that such indiscriminate promiscuity does not accord with his character, and would want his lovemaking to have special meaning. So, he would wait for opportunities that would enrich rather than demean him.

Our only ambition will be to live our brief life to the utmost. We will leave the unfathomable questions of religion and philosophy to the priests and gurus. We must seek to find our own truth and our own place, and be free from the burdens of irrational opinions.

Only by striving for a life of happiness will we truly begin to appreciate the essential meaning of our existence. As the great American thinker Robert G. Ingersoll said:

Happiness is the only good.
The place to be happy is here.
The time to be happy is now.
And the way to be happy
is to make others so.

So, our goal is happiness, and if we live life nobly, with the good of others always in our heart, happiness will surely follow. And if we do this, as well as always striving to appreciate the best things in life, we will attain happiness not only for ourselves but for others, too. It becomes a self-perpetuating cycle, a wonderful wheel of life.

We must place the act of sexual congress in this context, too, for love is a sure and essential route to happiness. The fusion of our body with that of another is a perfect ecstasy that takes happiness to another sphere and transforms it, like magic, into bliss. Lovemaking that is mindful of the needs of your lover, as well as your own desires, is lovemaking that feeds the soul and nourishes the spirit.

Tantric sex

Tantra is an ancient philosophy that exalts sex as a means of connecting with the higher forces. The practitioners of Tantric sex aim to unite two lovers in one continuous stream of energy. Tantra challenges the modern concept of sexual experience as being focused on the genitals and on performance. The sexual rituals of Tantra aim instead to unite the whole body, mind and heart of the participants

Tantric sex is highly ritualized, involving cleansing and the eating of sacred meals. Some forms of Tantra demand the deliberate breaking of taboos and the eating of forbidden foods.

BELOW Tantra is an open philosophy that gay people can embrace wholeheartedly in their quest for sexual fulfilment.

Tantric sex has become popular in the West as a means of overcoming many of the fears and inhibitions that restrict or spoil sexual expression for so many people. It can also help rekindle sexual and emotional interest in couples who have been together for many years and who may have grown apart or become indifferent to each other.

We will include some elements of Tantra in this book, but for a fuller exploration you should seek out specialist practitioners (of whom there are an increasing number) who can help you to a more profound understanding of this particular philosophy.

The gay experience

The aim of this book is to encourage the reader to consider the integration of sexual expression into the whole person. This is essential for everyone, but for gay men it has taken on a much more profound importance.

The *Kama Sutra*'s message is that virtue, prosperity and eroticism are intimately and mutually interdependent. It tells us that sexual pleasure is not a simple thing, but has cosmic significance and is the route to enlightenment. Erotic desire is the energy of the universe.

Sex can place individuals in extraordinarily complex situations. Therefore, in order to avoid unpleasantness or unwelcome difficulties, these forces must be studied, practised and respected. The aim is to enhance and increase sexual pleasure to the point that the mega-orgasmic experience leads to life-changing emotional, spiritual and social insights. The techniques of pleasure revealed in the *Kama Sutra* even purport to open a window into the divine for those who use them correctly.

ABOVE Throughout history, all cultures have contained a wealthy privileged class that has had the time, the opportunity and the inclination to explore every avenue of sexuality.

Sex is easily available in gay circles. You can find it, with minimal effort, at all times and in all forms. Just about any man can go to a gay bar or a cruising area and get some kind of sex. But sexual relief is not the same as sexual satisfaction. Simply 'having sex' is not the same as making love, and while rushing to a quick, anonymous orgasm may bring immediate relief, it is unlikely to add much to a man's happiness quotient. Centuries of persecution and stereotyping have damaged many gay men's perception of themselves. We often internalize this negative view and feel that our sexual impulses are unclean, unworthy and even wicked. No wonder, then, that many gay men have reacted against this image by living a life of excess, perhaps involving hundreds of sexual partners each year. For all its apparent bounty, such a sex life excludes many men from experiencing a real, human connection with their partners. It can lead to the development of cynicism, emptiness and contempt for oneself and for those who do not immediately provide instant gratification, but who might – with

ABOVE If a man has developed his full potential in the way the *Kama Sutra* suggests, middle and old age need not be something to fear.

some patience and encouragement – provide something much more rewarding.

Casual and uncommitted encounters can be exciting, but if that's all there is, boredom inevitably follows. Those who are sexually compulsive can be overwhelmed eventually by unhappiness and a sense of emotional isolation, and once the skills of emotional connection have been lost, they are not easily recovered. For someone who lives a life of such dissipation, the passing of youth becomes a major crisis, which all too often leads to a lonely and bitter middle and old age. Everyone desires youth, but only those who have invested in themselves emotionally and spiritually will be rewarded by love in later life, too.

So, what we are concerning ourselves with here is not quantity, but quality. As the self-esteem of gay people rises, so does their expectation of a better quality of life. While a fully committed life partner may not be the ideal for all, every man should strive to experience at least one serious love affair before he dies.

Integrating our sexuality into our whole being

The fusion of sex into the wholeness of our lives has, until relatively recently, been very difficult for gay men. Sexual expression for homosexuals was often completely separate from every other aspect of life. Because of its illegality and the social stigma it attracted, gay love was traditionally surrounded by secrecy, denial and oppression. Until the latter part of the twentieth century most gay men were doomed never to find love of any kind.

For those lucky enough to live in big cities – and who were bold enough to search for it – there was usually a sexual underground, where some kind of clandestine sex life could be located.

Even now, many gay men remain hidden and furtive. They find sex through cruising in dirty and dangerous places such as tea-rooms, cottages, backrooms in sleazy bars and public parks. The sex obtained in these circumstances is, necessarily, rushed, stressful and anonymous. It often feels like little more than an extended session of masturbation.

Some men who engage in this kind of secretive sex claim that it is exciting simply because it is so dangerous, and even though they live integrated lives elsewhere, they still seek out the thrill of casual and uncommitted contact as a variation.

Although cruising and brief, public sexual encounters are still commonplace in every part of the world, something has happened that has released many men from this trap of estrangement from their own sexuality. It is called gay liberation.

The story of the gay movement – which is brief in terms of human history – has been well chronicled, but since the 1960s, the rebellion of homosexuals who were tired of lies, subterfuge and deceit has resulted in a profound change of self-image and a cultural shift of seismic proportions.

In cultures where women are confined, a form of homosexuality among young men might thrive, but this is merely the relief of frustration that would prefer to find its expression in heterosexuality if it were available. Earlier cultures legitimized

BELOW Erotic subjects were popular for the decoration of plates and vases in ancient Greece. Here, a seated man fondles his tyro. Many of these decorated objects were destroyed by some of the more repressive cultures that followed.

ABOVE In cultures where women are confined and secluded, otherwise heterosexual men will seek relief with other men. In such cultures a special contempt is reserved for men who allow themselves to be penetrated.

homosexual expression in some circumstances, but in those times, gay relationships were restricted and formalized, and often rested on customs such as the sytem of mentoring of young men by older men, as existed in ancient Greece and Rome. Love of a sort might have been involved, but the concept of these relationships being permanent, widespread or an alternative to the heterosexual model was simply unthinkable. Once the youths in these partnerships had matured into adulthood, they were expected to marry and procreate in the usual tradition. Their mentors/lovers were already married.

Now, for the first time in history, it is possible – in Western culture at least – for two men to enjoy a relationship intended to be exclusive and lifelong. The concept of the 'gay man' has been born.

The idea of a homosexual 'orientation', or a state of mind that dictates that a man feels sexual attraction and loving impulses towards members of his own sex exclusively, was unimaginable until the last century. Now, it is widely accepted as reality.

True homosexual orientation means that a man not only seeks his sexual partners among other men, but he seeks to express his impulse to love and cherish in the same way. He sees his life partner as male.

In the West, two men or two women can form a bond of love and commitment, and can now do so publicly, often with the full approval of their family and friends, and increasingly within the framework of a legally sanctioned partnership structure.

Because gay life has emerged from a subculture of secrecy, it has developed in a haphazard fashion, without rules of behaviour being imposed from institutions such as the churches. The possibilities for relationships are, therefore, many and varied and there are no preconceived expectations about how we will live.

The concept of legally sanctioned 'gay marriage' has only recently been introduced, so there is, as yet, no cultural expectation that we will automatically participate in it. At present, it is just another option from a sometimes bewildering menu of possibilities.

Gay couples form unions of many kinds. Some stay together for decades, striving to find happiness as a unit as well as individuals. Others engage in serial monogamy, enjoying a relationship while it is fruitful and then moving on to the next when it ceases to be. Others choose to live singly and take their loves where they find them.

BELOW In some countries in the West, legalized partnership registrations give gay couples rights similar to those granted to men and women when they marry.

Now is the time to embrace our new opportunities for happiness and to challenge the residual feelings of guilt, shame and self-hate that still afflict so many of us. The *Kama Sutra* enjoins us to do just that: to ennoble ourselves through learning and to know ourselves through love. Most gay men can seize sexual opportunities with alacrity, but this book seeks to take the experience a stage further for those who want to make sex a much more enriching and fulfilling experience, one that is fully integrated into our whole being.

It will joyfully encourage love and sex, pleasure and sensuality, uninhibited erotic indulgence and play in the context of mutual respect and with the aim of bringing happiness as well as orgasms. It will also provide some insights into the philosophy of Tantric sex, and, for those who seek it, that promised window into the divine.

Raising self-esteem

If we are to conquer negative feelings about our sexuality, we need to raise our sexual self-esteem. By examining the ways in which society, religion, our parents and our teachers have caused us to feel bad about our sexuality, we can challenge our doubts.

We should be certain that what we feel for other men is legitimate, valuable and the road to achieving personal happiness. To do this, we have to see our gayness in a new, positive light.

Sometimes, as we move in gay circles, we see destructive behaviour that makes us feel bad about ourselves. We have already looked at the way some men obsessively rush from one sexual conquest to the next and come to regard other men merely a means to an end.

But this is not the whole truth about being gay. We can choose not to embrace that style of hedonism that often results in disillusionment, disease and a lack of respect for humanity.

Open heart, healthy love

• Let us, who are seeking supreme happiness in sex rather than mere gratification, resolve to change the way we regard ourselves, and those with whom we make love.

• Let us seek out positive role models – men who love life, embrace their wholeness, respect their fellow men and see lovemaking as a joy to savour and a means of fusing with humanity, rather than just a pursuit of lust.

• Let us educate ourselves about our sexuality, reading extensively from the vast body of literature that has accumulated about our history, our politics, our struggles and our triumphs. There are reassuring volumes that can tell us that being gay is no tragedy and, despite the myths with which we have been inculcated since our earliest days, that we are neither evil nor perverse for feeling as we do about other men.

• To help us in our search for relationships of equality, we should familiarize ourselves with the theory of assertiveness. There are hundreds of books on this topic, and they will provide some insight into our behaviour and how we treat other people. The art of love is also the art of communication, and assertiveness provides the tools for more effective and honest exchanges between people.

• Let us try positive reinforcement. The mind will eventually accept a message that is repeated. We can improve the way we think about ourselves and our desires by creating brief, uplifting messages about our sexuality and repeating them each day. For instance, 'Being gay is a positive aspect of my life', 'I will value and explore my sexuality' or 'My loving impulses are good and expressing them will bring me happiness', 'I will treat those to whom I make love with respect and empathy.' We might even write our own affirmations on a piece of paper and stick it to the shaving mirror so that we will see them and repeat them each day.

The male sexual impulse

Although our aim will be the creation of sexual experiences that gratify not just our senses but also our spirit, we have to be realistic. Gay men are, first and foremost, men, and their sexual impulses will not easily be tamed. A vigorous man who has been deprived of sexual outlet for any length of time can find the resulting pressure unbearable. This is as true for gay men as it is for straight men. Scientists have noted that healthy men who are deprived of sex often find it difficult to concentrate on anything else until they have found relief. They become edgy, bad-tempered and distracted. In these circumstances, slow and sensuous lovemaking might have to give way to the urgent and rough variety. Sometimes a rush to achieve climax is enough.

Men are quicker to sexual arousal than women and so, when two men are involved in a sexual encounter, it can take discipline and practice to slow the whole process down. We will explore the urgent and the protracted versions of sex, and combinations of the two. We will also look at ways in which partners who have been together for a period of years can rekindle and sustain the initial passion they felt for each other.

Sexual heroes

In the imagery that constantly bombards gay men through advertising, magazines and pornography, the ideal to which we are encouraged to aspire is unmistakable: a youthful, perfectly formed and proportioned body with a slim waist and broad shoulders, a well-developed musculature and – of course – a big dick. A pretty or handsome face is also necessary to complete the picture. Only the lucky few can fit that ideal.

Such paragons of perfection do exist, and occasionally we see them walking down the street and we sigh. But gorgeous men who may look like gods are just human like the rest of us, and while they may be desirable for sex – or maybe just sexual fantasy – they may still be intolerable as human beings.

A beautiful face is no guarantee that its possessor is an unselfish lover or a charming companion. Arrogance, callousness and bad breath are not restricted to the plain and ordinary; and thoughtfulness, concern and generosity can be cultivated by anyone.

For sex to have long-term meaning, a pretty face and a toned body are not enough on their own. Once the sex is over, you may want to hold your partner in a loving embrace – perhaps for the whole night. It will be difficult to feel such loving impulses towards someone who is concerned only with his own needs.

A sexual hero, then, may have a handsome face, he may have a bubble butt and a penis like a horse's, but he won't remain a hero for very long if he does not know how to make his lover feel desired and, more importantly, his equal.

A true sexual hero is someone who can charm his way into your affection, whatever his physical attributes (or lack of them). A man who wouldn't attract a second glance in a crowded room may have the skills of a true romantic. He may be able to seduce you with his voice alone, or as a caring and attentive lover. Someone who gains his pleasure from your pleasure is worth his weight in rubies.

Men come in all shapes and sizes, and in varying degrees of physical fitness and well-being. We all have our preferences for the type of man who attracts and arouses us. Here are some of the physical types that you are likely to encounter during your erotic journey through gay life.

BELOW What has been regarded as the ideal male physique has changed little over the centuries. Perhaps Michelangelo's *David* is still the ultimate rendition in art of masculine beauty.

THE BEAR. This man is acutely aware of his maleness and he takes pride in displaying his obvious masculine attributes. His body will be heavy and thickset and very hairy, his face will be large, with a prominent jaw and deep-set eyes. He will have trouble remaining clean-shaven for long, and however many times a day he may shave, the stubble will never be completely eradicated. Sometimes he will have a moustache or beard.

These unmistakably manly characteristics will become even more pronounced as the Bear matures. He accentuates his sexual persona through his clothing, which may include leather or denim. He often opens his shirt to display a big chest, thickly covered in hair. His hands will be large and strong, often calloused from physical work. His movements will be slow and measured, and he will carry himself with assurance – even with a touch of arrogance. For this is a man who knows he is a man and could never be mistaken for anything else, but this does not mean that he is incapable of great gentleness in intimate moments. Indeed, although Bears are often into the heavier kinds of sexual excitement such as S&M or corporal punishment, many are also very capable of gentleness and even passivity at other times.

THE ANTELOPE. Antelopes are at their best in their twenties, when the litheness and smoothness of their bodies are at their peak. They are built for speed and manoeuvrability, with light, but firm muscling. Perhaps they like to swim or play a sport that depends on speed and rapid reflexes – soccer is one of their favourites.

Their sleekness belies a hidden strength and they possess great stamina. As lovers they will be persistent and lovemaking sessions

BELOW In younger men, the the distinct characteristics of a physical type tend to be more instantly recognizable. However, as we grow older and our bodies inevitably change, these can be less easy to identify and we must learn to emphasize our other charms.

with these men will be extended and demanding. They are particularly suited to the more acrobatic sexual positions where suppleness is important.

Antelopes are very difficult to hold down, and they will range far and wide in their search for sexual adventure and new pastures. The maintenance of long-term relationships is not the antelope's strong point, so if you are to share pleasure with one, then you will have to accept that he will also probably be seeking different excitements elsewhere.

THE LION. The lion is strong and physically intimidating. He is the proverbial tower of strength, the Hercules of huge and rock-hard muscles. Often, this exaggerated physique is obtained by years of work in the gym, building on an already massive frame. It may also owe something to the injudicious use of steroids.

Such a 'man-mountain' is cumbersome at times, but his superbly developed body with the promise of extraordinary strength and forcefulness can hold great attraction. His face is often fixed in an expression of suspicion and challenge, which some can find intimidating. Life is a serious business for the Lion and he will not be noted for his humour.

As with the lion on the plains of Africa, you need to treat this man with caution, for his monstrous strength and occasional ferocity may one day be used to dominate you in ways that you do not enjoy. A tamed lion, though, can be loyal and protective. He will defend his territory and his mate against all threats, with fearsome determination. This can be extremely appealing to some people, while for others it would be unbearably restrictive.

THE SNAKE. The tall, elegant, slim figure of the Snake is recognizable by a long neck and long limbs. His musculature is light, and his body not particularly well contoured. His shoulders, waist and hips may be narrow, his buttocks small and, sometimes, flat, but that seems proportionate and right.

A narrow, longish face that often carries a look of handsome enigma usually accompanies his sinuous body. You will find yourself hypnotized by his eyes. He makes a great seducer, and his deep voice is a great asset when it comes to persuading you to get into his bed. He moves slowly but purposefully, and his movements, too, are as mesmerizing as his eyes. His body will be primed for even the most convoluted sexual enterprise.

THE CHEETAH. This man will retain a youthful build throughout his life, willowy, slight and with more than a touch of androgyny. In Indian mythology, androgyny was considered divine, and many of the deities are often represented as being half male and half female. The most notable example of this is Shiva, who is often depicted with a female left side and a right male side and in this form is called Ardnarishvara.

The Cheetah's body and face will be free from hair, or the hair that he does have will be soft and downy. His face will be smooth and pretty rather than handsome, with large, questioning eyes. For all their innocence, those eyes will speak of the promise of a thousand pleasures to come. The Cheetah seems too lightweight to be threatening, but this is misleading. As a lover, the Cheetah will give you all the pleasure of innocent youth with the depth of eroticism of an experienced lover.

Preferences

These five physical types describe the basic models, but they come in myriad variations. One type can also take on some of the characteristics of another. Some men allow themselves to go to seed and develop fat rather than muscle, and then it is difficult to determine to which category they belong.

Most of us have preferences when it comes to the shape and size of the men that attract us, but we should not become fixated on particular features. If we limit ourselves to one particular type of man – perhaps he 'must' have blond hair or a perfectly toned body, or it is 'essential' he be cut or uncut – then we are restricting our opportunities for loving and enriching sexual experiences.

BELOW In ancient Greece, artists depicted athletes with small genitalia – it was considered more aesthetically pleasing. In real life, though, the larger phallus was still highly regarded.

It is good to be excited by individual parts of the body, but we should try to avoid becoming too narrowly focused, to the extent that they exclude other delights.

Many gay men spend large amounts of time at the gym developing and perfecting the contours of their body. Vatsyayana, as we have seen, encourages this as one of the virtues that go to make up the whole. But he cautions restraint, in that the acquisition of the body beautiful is only a single aspect of being a perfect lover. The other virtues must be developed, too, in order to maintain the all-important balance. Being young, beautiful and well proportioned will certainly make sexual conquests easier, but that is not our sole purpose. Sexual couplings should have a higher purpose than mere gratification.

Safer sex and condoms

Anal intercourse is the act most likely to transmit HIV and therefore it is essential that condoms are employed at all times when fucking. This is the only known way, other than abstaining from this activity and finding alternatives, to prevent HIV entering the body.

The only time it is acceptable not to use condoms is when you are fucking or being fucked by a long-term partner whose health status you are absolutely certain of (and which is HIV-negative, like your own). At all other times, condoms are essential.

Some people regard condoms as a nuisance and a restraint. They say they remove the spontaneity from lovemaking, and diminish the sensation. But these reservations can be largely overcome. Make condoms an exciting part of your foreplay, eroticizing them and using them almost as a means of furthering your worship of the *lingam*.

Make a ceremony of helping your partner put on the condom, and lovingly anoint it with lubricant in preparation for the consummation of your love. But be careful not to get lubricant inside the condom, as this can cause it to slip off during sex.

Do not despise the condom or allow yourself to be taken in by the blandishments of those that say it is not important, or that sex is 'better without it', for the condom is your one and only defence against a disease that will change your life – and not for the better. Don't be seduced by the idea that the new drugs that are available are a cure for HIV infection; they are not – they simply keep the virus in check for as long as you continue to take them. But the strict regimes involved in using these therapies can be complicated and arduous, requiring a discipline that few can maintain at all times. Going on holiday, sleeping late or any other change in your usual routine can result in an interruption of the regime and undermine the drugs' effectiveness.

BELOW Sometimes a lover is slow to arousal and needs to be persuaded and cajoled. A skilled lover will eventually be able to awaken the ardour of his suitor, however indifferent he was at the beginning.

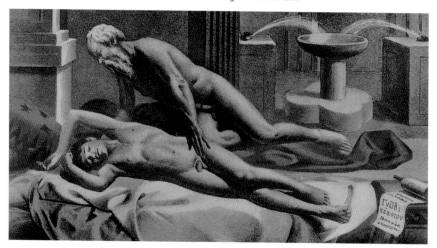

The anti-HIV medication regimes interfere with normal living, and sometimes the drugs, wonderful as they are, have undesirable and unpleasant side effects, such as lipoatrophy – or wasting – when body fat disappears from the face and buttocks.

ABOVE Condoms, now an essential part of gay life, are the only known protection against HIV infection and should be used at all times during penetrative sex.

You may think that having sex without condoms is striking a blow for freedom and spontaneity, but this freedom comes at a price – and that is a life sentence of pill taking and anxiety about every infection and malady from which you suffer. Each cold or rash could herald the development of AIDS, and that could mean the beginning of the end.

Combination therapies are not guaranteed to work for ever, nor can anyone guarantee that they will be available for ever. The body can become immune to the drugs, and then another regime has to be started. The drugs can be toxic in their own right, gradually poisoning the body over a period and shortening your life.

To avoid the disruptive and stressful consequences of HIV infection, make sure that you learn the rules of safer sex and discipline yourself to enforce them at all times in your love life. Bear in mind that you are likely to become irresponsible when under the influence of alcohol or illegal drugs, and so make your preparations before you set out on your erotic search. Always have condoms with you, and some lubrication. Don't leave responsibility entirely with your partner.

Be assertive in your love life. Never allow yourself to be seduced by those who wish to have penetrative sex with you without protection. You are an equal partner in any encounter, and you are as responsible as he is for ensuring that HIV does not become a dominating part of your life.

If you already have an HIV infection, there is a particular onus on you to ensure that you do not pass it on. Behave responsibly with your lovers. Discourage recklessness when you come across it, and always, always use condoms if you are planning anally penetrative sex.

Being HIV positive need not mean an end to your erotic life, but if you love and respect those with whom you make love, then you will want to spare them infection.

There are many and varied ways of enjoying a sexual experience that do not involve anal penetration, and you should exploit these to the full. But it has to be accepted that anal sex has a special meaning and creates a unique intimacy for many gay men, so ensure that condoms are employed at all times when you enter your partner anally.

ABOVE It's clear from historical artefacts that in most cultures penetration was seen as the likely outcome of a gay sexual encounter. Today, however, there are many alternative forms of lovemaking that will reduce the risk of HIV infection.

And remember, there is more than one strain of this virus. If you already have one strain, do not lay yourself open to another by imagining that because you are HIV positive it no longer matters whether you have protected sex with others who are HIV positive.

HIV and AIDS support organizations are easily located through gay media and help lines, and they produce informative leaflets that will bring you the latest thinking on safer sex. If you are unsure, arm yourself with knowledge, and resolve to put that knowledge into practice.

Research shows that rates of HIV among gay men are beginning to increase again, particularly in those under 25. This indicates that the safer sex message is being disregarded. But if you are to be a gay man who seeks the happiness and wholeness that we are exploring in this book, you will not join this growing band of imprudent young people who risk a foreshortened and unpleasant

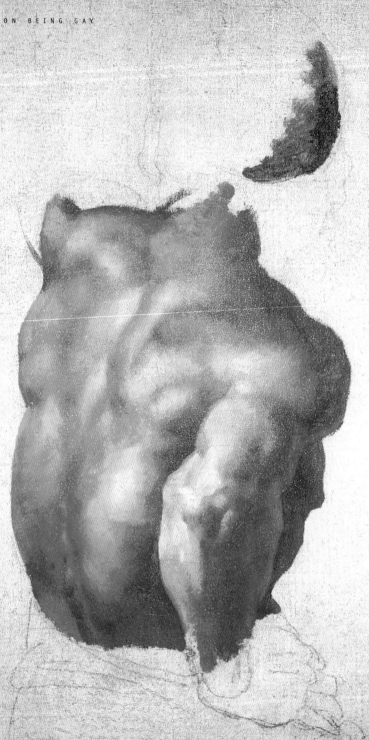

life by taking foolish risks. Your care for your own health will be matched by your concern for that of your lovers. Barebacking (anal sex without protection) is not for those with gay self-respect, only for idiots and the suicidal.

Familiarize yourself with condoms, play with them and masturbate with them on so that you become used to the sensation. Ensure that you use them by the date on the packet, and that they are from a reputable manufacturer.

To ensure that the condom fits properly, always wait until your erection is completely hard before putting it on. Then, holding the tip of the condom between your finger and thumb, squeeze the air out so that there is room for the semen, and unroll it all the way down to the base of your cock with the other hand.

After you have ejaculated, withdraw carefully while your cock is still hard and make sure to hold on to the base of the condom so that it doesn't slip off. Wrap it in a tissue as it might otherwise be difficult to flush away.

Condoms with bobbles, toggles, ribbing and other features ('ticklers' as they are sometimes called) may seem tempting, but they are often of poor quality, so resist. Also, don't buy the kind impregnated with spermicide, as this has been shown possibly to increase the risk of HIV transmission.

Condoms do not offer 100 per cent protection from HIV. They can tear, leak and slip off during intercourse, but – other than complete abstinence from penetrative sex – they are the best safeguard that we have at the moment. They not only offer some protection against HIV, but can also shield against other sexually transmitted diseases such as syphilis, herpes and gonorrhea, which we will look at in more detail later.

OPPOSITE The power of the male body, exhibited through a well-defined musculature, has inspired artists – gay and straight – throughout the ages. This image of a broad back evokes a keen sense of vigour and strength.

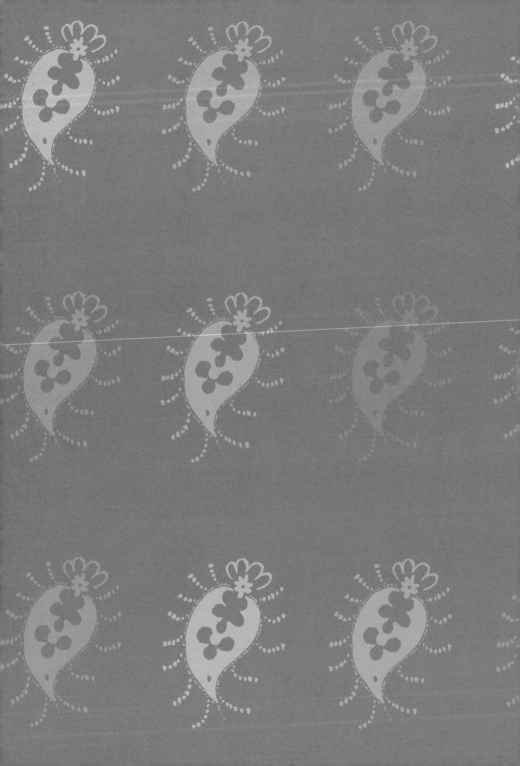

Chapter 2:
On preparing
for love

seduction and foreplay

seduction and foreplay

Knowing the workings of your own body will help you pleasure that of your lover. And being familiar with the wiles of seduction and foreplay will ensure that you and your partner gain maximum pleasure from your encounter.

ABOVE The handle of this Indonesian kris – or dagger – shows how the phallus is venerated and represented in art throughout the world's cultures.

OPPOSITE Poussin's study of Castor and Pollux, the mythological twins, provides once more an opportunity for a joyful depiction of the male form in all its youthful vitality.

Parts of the male body

Penis

In gay lovemaking, though we may take pleasure from other parts of the body, all worship is directed towards the lingam. Shiva, the most popular of all Hindu gods, has traditionally been worshipped primarily in the form of the lingam. In the most common ritual, milk is poured over the tip of the lingam and flows down on all sides.

Though our lingam is the focus of much energy, Tantra tells us that sex that is focused exclusively on the genitals and on the rush to orgasm will not ultimately prove to be the most satisfying.

Lovemaking should be a whole-body experience, and, ideally, will also engage the mind and the spirit to create a perfect circle of divine energy that will fuel our relationship.

RIGHT This fresco of a faun was found in the Roman city of Pompeii. Fauns were woodland deities in Roman mythology renowned for their sexual rapacity – and playing the pan-pipe of course.

In some sexual encounters, there may be a delicious suspense before contact is made with the genitals, but in most instances, for gay men, the lingam will be the first port of call. This is the moment that has been most anticipated, and few can resist reaching for their partner's most precious and private gift once it is clear that a sexual encounter is under way.

Usually, protracted foreplay, in which genital contact is deferred to increase excitement, is reserved for longer, more relaxed sessions with experienced lovers.

Of course, there are many sources of sensual pleasure on the body – erogenous zones – but it is the phallus that is most desired, and the urge to touch and fondle it will be irresistible.

Penises come in an endless array of shapes and sizes, as well as colours. The *Kama Sutra* categorizes penises according to size as 'the Horse', 'the Bull' and 'the Hare'. Of course, there are endless variations in size and the three categories can provide only a rough guide.

It is useful to know how the penis is constructed and how it works. The penis (a Latin word meaning 'tail') is a complicated organ, consisting of three spongy cylinders surrounding the urethral tube (through which urine and semen pass). When stimulated, the spongy tissue in the penis becomes engorged with blood, causing it to become stiff and erect. Powerful muscles at the base prevent a reverse flow of blood and help maintain the erection for as long as required.

The head, or glans, of the penis is, in most cases, covered by the foreskin or prepuce. In some uncircumcised men the foreskin is very long, but in others it is quite short. Both kinds – and everything in between – are perfectly normal. The underside of the glans is where the nerve endings that provide the pleasure are situated, and so it should be given a great deal of attention during oral sex.

The prepuce can usually be pulled back and forth over the head of the penis when it is in its relaxed state. If it cannot, then a condition called phimosis may be present. If this is a problem for you, don't try to force the foreskin over the glans if it won't go – it could be difficult to get it back again, causing a condition called paraphimosis, which could require surgery. If a tight foreskin is a problem, you could consider circumcision, although before proceeding, you will need to discuss all the implications of this with your physician.

Some penises have a bend in them, which may be quite pronounced. This is quite natural, and is nothing to worry about in most cases. If the bend is severe, however, it may indicate Peyronie's disease, symptoms of which include pain when the penis is erect and a hardened area caused by a fibrous tissue pulling the penis out of shape.

BELOW Priapus was the Roman god of gardens, wine-makers and sailors. He is usually depicted – as here – with an enormous, erect penis.

Many men are anxious about the size of their penis, considering it to be 'too small'. But if their cock is smaller than average (about 6 inches/15 centimetres when erect), it does not mean that it is inferior from the point of view of obtaining or giving pleasure. All penises, whatever their size, have the same number of nerve endings, and so the potential for pleasure is the same whether it is small or large.

In the USA, researchers measured the flaccid (unerect) penises of 7,239 men. The largest in the survey was 5 inches (13 centimetres) from the root, the smallest $2^1/_4$ inches (6 centimetres) – the average was just under 4 inches (10 centimetres). The researchers found that the smaller penises were capable of greater expansion.

There's no question that the gay media and pornography glorify and overemphasize the penis, and this has encouraged some men to become neurotic about the size of their own. We are constantly bombarded with photos of men with fantastically bulging jock straps and underwear, and we look at adult movies featuring men of quite extraordinary proportions. This can make us feel jealous and inadequate. But we should bear in mind that actors in these movies are chosen because they aren't average. They are there to fulfil a fantasy.

Not only does the size of penises vary greatly, so does every other aspect of their appearance. Circumcised penises can look very different from uncircumcised; some are smooth and silky while others have bulging veins; some are pink; some are brown; others are a combination of several colours – pale on the shaft and livid red on the head, with very prominent blue veins; some are long, thin and cigar-shaped; others are broad and stumpy with a pronounced 'knob' at the end.

LEFT Priapus was a very popular god with the Romans, who would put his image – complete with monstrous phallus – in their gardens to encourage fruitfulness. This version is part of a fresco in Pompeii.

When you are preparing for a first-time sexual encounter with a new lover, there is a glorious anticipation about what he may produce. He may be a Horse or he may be a Hare, but it is important that we do not judge him purely on his penis. Be thankful if he turns out to be a Horse, but do not revile him if he is a Hare. Who knows what other erotic delights he may have in his repertoire?

Remember, our aim is to maximize the pleasure of our sexual contacts, and this will not be done by judging your potential partner – your fellow human being – solely on the size of his penis. To do so would be to create a separation between you, and you will never reach the heights of pleasure you might have done had you chosen to treat all human beings with respect and equality.

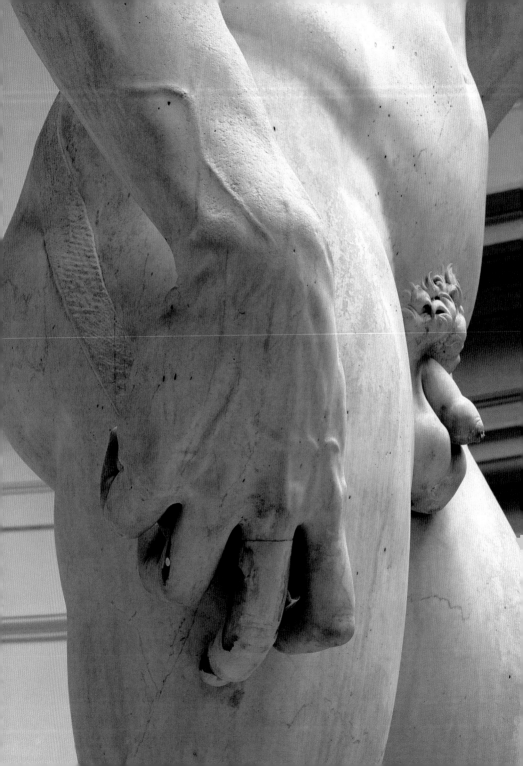

So here we have the first rule of transcendent love: give your partner the respect that any fellow human being deserves – do not humiliate him or judge him on his physical attributes or on his lack of knowledge or experience.

If you can introduce this concept into your encounter, and leave behind the urge to dismiss and sneer, then you will find that the potential for something special to happen is increased. Your partner is more likely to respond in a positive way, with the result that both of you can proceed to heights of ecstasy that would be impossible were one of you to regard the other with contempt and disdain.

OPPOSITE The male genitalia varies greatly in size and shape between individuals. Worry about what is 'normal' creates much unnecessary anxiety among men, sometimes leading to performance difficulties.

The balls

The testes or balls (called *jaghanabbag* in the *Kama Sutra*) are a primary sexual characteristic and therefore an important part of the erotic experience. A handsome pair of balls, contained within their scrotal sac, can make an appealing sight. Like the penis, they come in many varieties. Some are small and close to the body, others are heavy and hang low, and swing most attractively when liberated by pelvic thrusts. The left is usually slightly larger than the right and hangs lower (the opposite is true of left-handed men). The scrotal sac is usually hairy.

The primary function of the testes is to manufacture sperm and the hormone testosterone, which is responsible for so many sexual characteristics of the male body. Their secondary purpose is to enhance pleasure during the lovemaking process.

The *jaghanabbaga* are sensitive, and much pleasure can be obtained from attending to them during lovemaking. Tickling, licking, sucking and cupping them in the hand are all likely to be pleasurable experiences for both partners.

Many men find that their balls are extra sensitive. They recoil involuntarily if anyone makes sudden grabbing movements towards them, and so it is important, especially with a new partner, always to let him know, either by word or gesture, that you intend to fondle his *jaghanabbaga*.

Once your partner trusts you, he will give you complete access to this area of great pleasure, and his flinching will stop. Some men have a greater tolerance for rough handling of the balls than others. Only by gradually increasing the strength of your grip will you discover your lover's tolerance level. Always relax your hold if he shows any sign of pain, discomfort or anxiety.

The pleasure of licking and sucking the balls can be intensified by holding an ice cube in your mouth or sipping champagne to fizz on him. Put a tiny bit of toothpaste on your tongue and lick his balls, then blow on them for a cooling effect.

The anus

This is another primary source of pleasure for gay men. Pert and rounded buttocks are highly prized among men who love men, although there are also fans of the smaller, flatter, less well-developed rear end. Caressing, massaging and kneading the buttocks are important precursors to the more intimate explorations that will soon follow.

The anus is regarded as a source of divine energy in Tantric sex, and is not be eschewed as a fount of profound pleasure. It contains many nerve endings, and responds well to massage by the fingers. This is often the overture to penetration, and the finger should be lubricated with a mild cream or jelly in order for insertion into the anus to be made more easily.

The sphincter muscle, which surrounds the anus, is strong and sometimes resistant. Pushing past it can initially cause pain, and it is important for the insertor always to be aware of his partner's reactions. If there is any indication of discomfort, gently ask whether you are hurting him. Then, after reassuring him, begin again, massaging the outside of the anus, gradually relaxing it before trying once more.

If you are inserting your fingers into the anus, it is essential that your nails are well trimmed and smooth. Jagged or sharp nails can cause damage to the delicate lining of the anus. Remove any rings that might have sharp edges.

If you are the receptive partner, you can, with experience, teach yourself to relax your sphincter muscle and therefore make the whole experience painless and pleasurable.

You do this by concentrating fully on your anus, closing your eyes and directing all your attention to the area that your lover is exploring with his fingers. Make a conscious effort to relax your buttocks and then to relax the sphincter. You have more control over it than you imagine.

If you are inexperienced, it may take several attempts before you can allow penetration without pain, but if you persevere, you will find that eventually the finger slides in easily, and your lover can pleasure you by gently thrusting it in and out. Soon he will be able to insert two, or even three fingers. Some men even insert the whole hand and forearm (fisting), but this a dangerous activity best avoided by those who value their health.

When he has pleasured you, and himself, with his fingers, your lover can then proceed to penetrate you with his lingam, which, now that the sphincter is relaxed, will enter more easily. Once he

has managed to insert his penis without causing you pain or distress, the potential pleasures of your lovemaking are boundless.

We will look at the many positions that can be enjoyed for intercourse later, but in the meantime, you should know something about the anatomy of your anus and rectum, and how to maintain and protect it.

Its most important function, of course, is the evacuation of waste material from the body, so it is important that cleanliness is maintained at all times when the anus is being used for sexual purposes. Some men like to douche before anal sex, which simply means squirting warm water into the rectum about an hour before you intend to begin your sexual activities. This helps to evacuate all waste material, after which you can shower and wash the area thoroughly. This presents your lover with a pristine orifice, which will give much pleasure and satisfaction. Douching or enema kits are obtainable from pharmacies and sex shops and over the Internet.

Douching is something that should be kept for special occasions, and not done regularly. The bacterial flora in the rectum and colon are finely balanced, and frequent douching may end up disturbing this balance, resulting in health problems. So, try to use plain water, only slightly warm, to achieve the effect. Add the mildest soap in very small quantities only if plain water does not work.

A clean anus should hold few dangers, but if not properly cleaned there is the possibility of infection. Hepatitis A, B and C can pass through this route, as well as several other parasitical diseases. It is, perhaps, advisable to reserve your anal pleasures for those whom you know well, and whose health status you are sure of. Otherwise, ensure that adequate protection is used at all times. The use of disposable surgical rubber gloves has proved satisfactory during stimulation by finger, allowing the maximum amount of sensation with a minimum of danger and restriction.

Anilingus, or rimming, is another occupation that many find appealing and delightful. It means licking and kissing the anus of your lover. It goes without saying that the strictest hygiene is necessary if you are undertaking this activity.

BELOW In gay sex, the anus is a primary focus of pleasure. Anilingus (oral–anal contact) is popular with many gay men, and can be enjoyed in many different positions.

Sufficient lubrication is necessary when penetration of the anus is involved. It is also essential that condoms are worn at all times for anal penetration by the penis, unless you are with a regular lover whose health status you are certain of. Ensure that you use only a water-based lubricant with condoms, as oil-based lubricants will quickly dissolve the rubber. (We will look at safer sex in more detail later.)

Further into the anus lies the prostate gland, a chestnut-sized organ that sits under the bladder, in front of the rectum. The prostate manufactures the seminal fluid, which carries the sperm when ejaculation takes place. The prostate is also very sensitive to touch, and manually stimulating it can bring great pleasure. Experienced lovers know where the prostate is situated and can use their fingers to massage it. To get there, slide a lubricated finger, encased in a condom or a surgical glove, about 2 inches (5 centimetres) inside your rectum. Move the end of your finger towards your belly button until you come to a bulge. That's it, but be careful to stroke gently, and don't poke or scratch. You may notice your penis reacting with jerks. Sometimes, this gentle massage is sufficient in itself to create an orgasm. The prostate has been called the male G-spot, and for good reason.

Swollen veins called haemorrhoids, which are often very painful, can affect the anus. Those suffering from this condition would be better advised to put the emphasis of their lovemaking on other parts of the body.

The nipples

Many men have extremely sensitive nipples, so pay full attention to them during lovemaking. Some men imagine that there is a nerve connecting the nipples with the glans of the penis, for when their nipples are stimulated, they feel sensations at the other end.

The nipples can be licked, sucked, gently bitten, pinched, rubbed with fingers or lingam and sometimes pinched hard with a sex toy called a tit clamp. Men react differently to tit play. Some like it hard and rough, while others find their nipples extremely sensitive and prefer gentler, more subtle stimulation.

In some men, the nipples can become very hard and erect when stimulated, while in others they will remain flat but still sensitive. Piercing the nipples to insert metal rings is also popular.

ABOVE Men's nipples are very sensitive and can play a great role in obtaining and giving sexual pleasure. The experienced gay lover will ensure that his partner's nipples are given a great deal of loving attention, including sucking, licking and gentle biting.

Other erogenous zones

There are many other erogenous zones on the body that react well to the tender (and the not so tender) ministrations of a lover. The feet are appealing to some men, and toe-sucking is common. Footwear and socks are a turn-on for others. Kissing, biting and scratching various sensitive parts of the anatomy are essential in love play. We will look more closely at what the *Kama Sutra* suggests later.

Body language

One of the arts that Vatsyayana recommends the rounded man to study is body language. This is the reading of unspoken desires and messages through the gestures, postures and facial expressions of the object of desire.

Modern psychology has refined the understanding of this language greatly and, with a little knowledge of these skills, it is possible to gain an insight into people's motivations, moods and intentions as well as their honesty, by carefully noting their non-verbal signals.

Much sexual body language appears to apply mainly to the interactions of men and women, but there are some signals that are easily applied to men. The signals that gay men exchange when they first meet and feel a shaft of erotic desire passing between them are often more direct.

In gay bars and clubs, there is less need to read body language. Everyone knows that everyone else is a potential partner, directness is the order of the day and staring in a way that would otherwise be regarded as intimidating or lascivious is permissible. Direct, unambiguous approaches to potential sexual partners are expected.

But if you are in a non-gay environment – say at a party organized by a straight friend – you will generally have to be more circumspect in your approaches. If you meet someone you find attractive, but whose sexuality or receptiveness you are unsure of, you can try to read the non-verbal signals that he is giving out.

Standing in close proximity to someone (invading their personal space) is a signal that increased intimacy is desired. So, if the object of your fancy is chatting to you, and he inches forward, closing the gap between you to, say, $1^1/2$ feet (half a metre) or less, it's safe to assume that he'd like to get closer.

You can try this the other way around: you could move in closer. If he moves back at the same time to maintain the distance between you, then he is signalling that he does not welcome your intimacy.

Eye contact is the signal that we all understand. If the two of you hold eye contact for more than a few seconds (particularly if you are not talking at the time), then it is a potential sign that you

ABOVE Learning to read non-verbal signals and gestures is an essential skill that all potential lovers should possess. Vatsyayana recognized 2,500 years ago that mastering body language helped in the art of seduction.

are on the right track. When you break the contact be sure to glance down quickly and discreetly at his crotch. This will indicate to him what your intentions are. Observe carefully to see whether he looks at your crotch at any point during the conversation.

Mirroring is another good way to tell whether you are making an impression. If you are both drinking, for example, he will sip from his glass at the same time that you sip from yours. If you are both seated and you cross your legs, he will cross his. When standing together, he will angle his body towards you. The technical term for this behaviour is 'building a rapport'.

Some signals will suggest that you are making no progress (either he's straight or he doesn't find you attractive). If he constantly glances over your shoulder while you are talking to him, angles himself away from you or folds his arms, crosses his legs away from you or maintains a distance of more than $1^1/_2$ feet (half a metre), he's not interested. If he says 'yes' to anything, but accompanies it with a tiny headshake, he may not be being straightforward. Hiding his mouth with his hands is another negative signal.

There are also positive signs to look out for. If he touches his lips soon after meeting you he is signalling sexual interest – coupled with anxiety about possible rejection. If he suddenly withdraws and gazes into the distance, he is unconsciously retreating to test if you will follow. Continue to flirt, even though he appears to have withdrawn. Watch also for dilation of the pupils of his eyes. The wider they become, the more turned on he is.

A smile is the universal signal of reassurance and friendliness. But smiles come in an enormous variety of styles, and human beings are skilled from childhood at reading the subtle differences.

So unless you are a very good actor, don't force your smiles – their insincerity will be obvious to all but the most insensitive.

There are many other signals to look out for, and it would be to your advantage to read a book about them. A man who can interpret body language, and use it to send subconscious signals, will be at a distinct advantage when it comes to pinpointing lovers.

Touch

As far as erotic pleasure is concerned, touch is one of the most important of the senses. When an encounter is promised, the first touch may simply be brushing by someone, as if by accident – or it may be a squeeze of the arm, which offers reassurance and friendship.

Hand-holding is something all lovers do, and the first touch of the hands of potential partners can be intensely exciting. If the first touches are slight strokes, maybe on the back of the hand

BELOW The *Kama Sutra* encourages the enjoyment of all five senses during lovemaking. The exploration and stimulation of all erogenous zones with the hands can push passion to new heights.

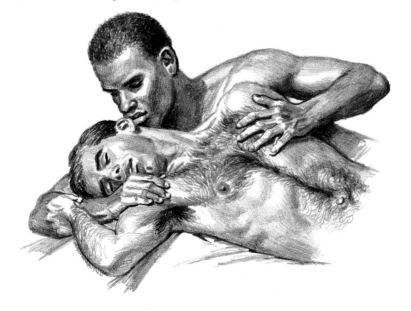

or on the palm, the lovers can signal to each other that they would welcome a greater involvement.

Gentle strokes upon the cheek and neck areas can also speak volumes about tender intentions.

These light touches and squeezes will eventually lead to more fervent embraces, and the *Kama Sutra* categorizes these as: rubbing, pressing and piercing.

Rubbing occurs when the lovers are walking together, and one slips his arm around the waist of the other and pulls him close, causing their bodies to rub together.

Pressing is when one lover pushes another against a pillar or wall and presses his body hard against him. This might also involve thrusting from the hips, imitating the movements of intercourse.

Piercing is when one lover has an erection underneath his clothes and presses hard against his lover so that he can feel the firmness against his own body. He may guide his lover's

ABOVE The initial embraces allow couples to press their bodies together and show their intentions during courtship, sometimes simulating sexual thrusting, or ensuring that the lover feels the erect penis against his body.

hand down to his excited penis and encourage him to fold his fingers over it These last two embraces are usually restricted to lovers who are aware of each other's intentions and represent a delicious overture and promise for later, and much more intimate, connections.

The embraces

Then come the embraces. *Jaghana* is that part of the body from the navel to the thighs, and the embrace named after that area involves you cupping your lover's buttocks and lifting him up so that you can bury your face in his thighs, planting kisses on his belly. You might, in these moments, gently bite, scratch, lick or suck the flesh as previously described.

The 'embrace of the breasts' involves lovers stimulating their nipples by sucking, licking and gently biting, and then when they are erect, pressing their chests together and further stimulating them by subtle movements.

The 'embrace of the forehead' involves one lover very gently kissing the forehead, brow and eyelids of the other. This is often saved for after lovemaking and before or during sleep. It is said to promote restful slumber and pleasant dreams.

The 'twining of the creeper' involves the lovers being closely entwined, even entangled, with legs and arms criss-crossing each other's bodies, one man with his head bent and the other gazing lovingly into his eyes, waiting to begin a long kiss.

The 'climbing of the tree' is when one lover places his foot upon his lover's foot and then his other foot on his thigh, while passing one arm around his back and the other over his shoulder. It seems he is trying to climb up his lover as he would climb a tree.

BELOW When lovers' embraces become more intimate, a complex crossing and interlocking of arms and legs is called in the *Kama Sutra* 'the mixture of sesame seed with rice'.

When the lovers lie down and are entwined closely with their arms and legs wrapped around each other, it is termed 'the mixture of sesame seed with salt'.

The 'flower duet' occurs at the very peak of ecstasy, when the lovers are in the act of intercourse, and are giving no thought to pain or any sensation other than that of sexual bliss. Their limbs are entangled in complicated ways, and they are both crooning with pleasure.

BELOW Vatsyayana's poetic descriptions of the many possible embraces that lovers can enjoy urge partners to deploy the imagination to full effect.

The different intensities of love

The *Kama Sutra* tells of the different levels of erotic love that depend on the intensity of the lovers' desires. Sometimes lovers are extremely excited and aroused, and in those circumstances the lovemaking is likely to be brief and turbulent. At other times their desire is only moderate, and it takes a little while to bring their passion to the boil. And then there are times when desire is low, and a lover can be reluctant even to consider sex.

We all experience these differing levels of intensity, and it is inevitable that of course that they will not always occur at the same time for both lovers.

A man who feels a strong urge to have sex may find that his lover does not, on that occasion, match his intensity. If they are regular lovers, they may accommodate each other – the one with the urgent need for relief, being indulged by the other, even though his own desires burn only moderately or hardly at all.

BELOW In this scene from mythology, the warriors are depicted as strong and handsome men – they were the heroes of their time and credited with great feats of daring and bravery. No doubt they featured in many a gay dream in ancient Greece.

For men, passion can be lit very easily, even at times when they were not thinking of sex. Evolution has made most men into sexual opportunists, and if an unexpected chance for an encounter presents itself, they can usually rise to the occasion.

So, a man whose mood is not ardent at first may find that with a little encouragement it flares quite dramatically. In that case, his passion may peak after

his lover's is spent. Once more, considerate partners will allow for that, and ensure that both are completely satisfied.

For the first encounter, love is likely to be brief and urgent. The lovers will hurtle towards the climax with wild desires and rapid thrusts. In this kind of lovemaking, there can be rough foreplay, fierce domination and an element of coercion. If one partner is particularly excited and is aroused to the point of unbearable passion, he can become aggressive and domineering, taking his pleasure selfishly. In these circumstances it is as well simply to succumb and enjoy this savage use of your body for the pleasure of your lover. In an equal, loving partnership, you will have your turn.

Sometimes in our busy world when time is short and the hours available for love are rationed, this will have to suffice. But if there is more time, the lovers can wait a short while before resuming their congress, the next time at a more leisurely and considered pace.

For men, the resting time needed between sexual encounters varies. For younger men it is short, and sometimes they can have three, four or more sexual episodes in one night. As they grow older, the recovery time, or 'refractory period', lengthens. It can take as little as half an hour or as much as three hours for desire to return to a level where an erection is possible and the action can resume.

There is something called a 'paradoxical refractory period', which occurs in older men, who may require 12 hours or more to attain an erection if foreplay has been interrupted and the erection lost before orgasm takes place.

For most men, the second and third sexual encounters within one extended session will be slower and more exploratory. It is during these more lingering encounters that the *Kama Sutra*'s many wiles will be even more useful in raising passion to a new height.

OPPOSITE Sometimes, perhaps after a period of separation, lovemaking is urgent and rough. At times like this, there is little point in trying to slow the process down – it's better to enjoy the passionate rush to orgasm.

Scratching and biting

Vatsyayana writes: 'No acts can be compared to scratching and biting for increasing amorous excitation and driving to action.' The *Kama Sutra* describes in great detail the forms of scratching, biting and slapping that can be employed.

It says that all parts of the body are suitable for biting, except for the upper lip, the tongue and eyes. Places that offer opportunities for use in these ways include the forehead, lower lip, neck, cheeks, chest and nipples, the sides of the body, the armpits, knees, thighs, calves, feet and toes. The sexual organs, too, can be used, but great care must be taken not to scratch or bite too hard, as these parts are sensitive and easily damaged.

Sometimes, the height of passion can feel almost unbearable, as though your chest or head will burst with excitement. It is at these times that scratching can be used as a means of releasing the intensity.

Pressing the nails into the flesh can create patterns to which the *Kama Sutra* gives romantic names, such as the half-moon, when one nail is pressed into the flesh, and the circle, when two nail impressions are made opposite each other.

Scratching and biting are often employed by lovers who have been reunited after a quarrel. The infliction of mild pain during the reconciliation can express something that words cannot.

The teeth are often used after kissing. Gentle nibbling of the ear lobes, lips, breasts, stomach and thighs may be so delicate as to leave no mark. Deeper kissing of the flesh and sucking at it will leave a small bruised area called a love bite. The *Kama Sutra* describes many types of bite, such as the hidden or discreet bite (*gudhaka*), which is where the lower lip is taken gently between the teeth and pressed. It is often so gentle that it leaves no sign.

The swollen or impressed bite (*ucchunaka*) is similar to the discreet bite, but is more forceful and leaves a slightly reddened mark. It is not restricted to the lips and may be used on hidden parts of the body. Patterns can be created, like a bouquet of flowers, perhaps on the buttocks or chest. These patterns have other names, such as 'scattered clouds' and 'the coral jewel'.

A bite called 'the chewing of the wild boar' (*varaha-charvita*) consists of making a ring of love bites around the genitals, creating a frame. The closer the love bites are to the penis, the wilder is the boar.

Vatsyayana says that only love play that increases arousal should be engaged in at first. Perhaps biting and scratching should be kept on a rudimentary level until later in the relationship. But varying the techniques can help your love endure.

ABOVE Elaborate and poetic instructions for love bites and kisses are described by Vatsyayana, and much pleasure can be had by placing these small tokens of passion on your loved one's most intimate places.

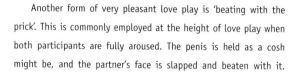

Another form of very pleasant love play is 'beating with the prick'. This is commonly employed at the height of love play when both participants are fully aroused. The penis is held as a cosh might be, and the partner's face is slapped and beaten with it.

Sometimes the one being beaten will try to catch the cock in his mouth, but his tormentor will not permit it, taunting and teasing him with blows on the forehead, cheeks and chin. The one being beaten may sometimes offer his tongue for similar treatment, allowing it to be slapped by the penis in the hope of catching a small taste of the desired object.

The buttocks can also be slapped with the penis as an overture to penetration (slapping can be hard and loud, causing the cheeks to flush pink).

Other slapping and punching techniques are described in the *Kama Sutra*, but we need not look at them in detail here as lovers in the throes of congress will know what pleases them; they will experiment and come to know each other's preferences.

Some lovers delight in slapping the buttocks with the hand. The strength of the blows will depend on the preferences of those involved. Some care only for gentle, playful slaps, while others desire something firm and vigorous that will leave a temporary impression in the flesh of the fingers and palm.

Rubbing

This is also much valued as a prelude to more intimate sexual union. Sometimes it can be a safer sex practice, used as an alternative to full penetration. The hand is a marvellously dexterous instrument, and the fingers are the focus of our sense of touch. The large number of nerves on the ends of our fingers allows us to feel shape, texture, temperature and even wetness in great detail. We can rub many parts of the body with our hands and fingers, and in its most organized form this is called massage.

You can lie on top of each other, belly-to-belly, and rub your genitals together, or you can rub your penis on other parts of the body. Lubrication makes rubbing against the hairier body parts more comfortable, but too much lubrication can dampen sensation.

Some men enjoy rubbing their penis on their partner's nipples, or between the buttocks on the anus without actually penetrating.

BELOW Hercules was a mythical hero of prodigious strength, and his legendary battle with the apparently invincible giant Antaeus is often depicted in art, giving the opportunity for much homoerotic suggestion.

Kissing

According to the *Kama Sutra*, kissing is a very important part of foreplay and, indeed, throughout history, kissing has been seen as an expression of serious intent. It is one of the first stages of lovemaking, and Vatsyayana tells us that there are various kinds of kiss that can be enjoyed at various stages of seduction, from the initial meeting through to full intercourse and its aftermath.

Begin with the most tender of kisses, one that brushes only lightly over the skin of the beloved's face. This kiss can be gently placed on the forehead, the eyes, the neck, the cheek or the ears. It will spark all kinds of longings and the urge for much more intimate contact.

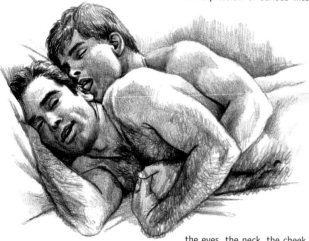

ABOVE Licking can provide exquisite sensations for both partners. The neck and ears are particularly sensitive to this form of attention.

RIGHT Kissing is a universal expression of love – and the more passionate the kiss, the more aroused the lovers are likely to be. The *Kama Sutra* describes the many types of kisses and the part they play in the increase of passion.

Later, the lovers will move on to the more passionate kisses that involve pressing the lips together, at first with mouth closed and then open with play of tongues. The lovers can explore the inner parts of each other's mouth with their tongues. When the tongue is sucked, it is called 'the soul kiss'.

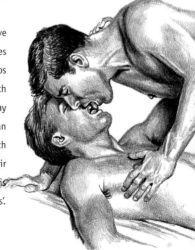

When passion increases, the lovers can enter the phase of the bliss kiss, when both tongues are urgently probing each other's mouths, and the tongues intertwine and fight. Kisses can be planted on all parts of the body, but they will provoke most sensation on the buttocks, neck, feet, shoulders and in the small of the back. Also sensitive are the backs of the knees, the armpits, nipples, abdomen and between the shoulders.

At first, lovers sometimes close their eyes when kissing, but later they will want to gaze lovingly into the eyes of their partner as their kisses become more intense.

Love talk

Some lovers prefer to enjoy their congress in silence, or to the accompaniment of non-verbal sounds such as moans, grunts and sighs. Others like to speak – or hear – what is known as 'dirty talk'. At the height of passion some people like to hear their lover speak crudely and directly about what they are doing or what they intend to do. Lovers can urge each other on to new heights with demands couched in the kind of sexual language that might be reserved only for these intimate moments. If it contributes to the raising of the sexual temperature, then 'dirty talk' should be unrestrained and even, in some cases, abusive in tone.

ABOVE The wild wrestling of tongues and the frenzied exploration of your lover's mouth and lips indicates a level of excitement that will be satisfied only by a full expression of sex, culminating in orgasm.

Chapter 3:
On making love

sexual positions

ABOVE This ancestral figure from New Guinea is another illustration of how the phallus has, throughout history, come to represent power and to symbolize male domination.

OPPOSITE Masturbation, most people's first experience of sexual delight, is a pleasure that the majority of men continue to practise throughout their lives – even by those who are in a permanent relationship.

Imagination and variation are the secret of successful lovemaking, but pleasure can be marred by anxiety over performance. An appreciation of the infinite varieties of sex should be accompanied by knowledge of the problems that can spoil it.

Masturbation

Don't listen to those who tell you stories of masturbators going blind, growing hair on the palms of their hands, or becoming weak or impotent. This is all propaganda perpetuated by those who sought, because of some misguided religious principle, to control and suppress sex of all kinds.

Masturbation is undoubtedly the most commonplace sex act in the world. It is the way in which we all first discover the joys of our sexual nature, and its practice stays with us throughout our lives, unless our sexual urges evaporate entirely. Even those who are sexually active with a partner will still occasionally seek release in masturbation. It is not disloyal to want privacy occasionally to

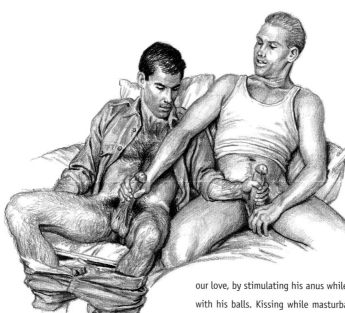

be with your own thoughts and fantasies.

Masturbation plays an important part in sex between two men. Mutual masturbation is a very common activity in gay lovemaking, and it can be undertaken to the accompaniment of many different stimuli. We can add to the pleasure of masturbation by sucking and licking the nipples of our love, by stimulating his anus while he masturbates, or by playing with his balls. Kissing while masturbating is enough to bring some men to climax.

The most usual way to bring a man to orgasm by hand is to grasp the erect penis and make pumping movements up and down the shaft, varying both the pressure of the hand and the speed of the movement. Applying a lubricant can also help create intense and gratifying sensations.

Solo masturbation is a matter of practice and preference. We will all have spent time finding the method that is right for us, and in the position we prefer. We can use other stimuli such as dildos, vibrators and pornography to enhance the experience.

There are no rules about what is the 'right' way to masturbate, or how many times a day is 'normal'. Young men who are at the height of their sexual desire might find that they need to

ABOVE Perhaps the most frequent expression of sex between men is mutual masturbation. It can be part of foreplay or the final act that leads to orgasm. It needs no preparation and can be performed in even the most restrictive of circumstances.

masturbate four or five times a day – that's OK. Your body will tell you when you've had enough.

Oral sex

Vatsyayana regards fellatio (or a 'blow job') as an inferior form of sex, but in the manuscripts that preceded the *Kama Sutra*, the ancient masters gave it greater respect. In some ancient Indian sex manuals, it was even regarded as a delightful variation for lovers. In the Western world it is a common form of sexual expression and in gay life it is almost universal.

An elaborate ritual of licking and tickling with the tongue can precede full oral sex. The shaft of the penis can be licked and stroked with the lips before the tongue attends to the tip, where most of the pleasure nerves are situated.

Inexperienced lovers will probably begin by taking only the end of the penis into their mouth, gently pressing the end of it with their lips. Later they will take the lingam further in

LEFT Oral sex is an important, often protracted, element of gay lovemaking, and skill in this art takes time to acquire. But bliss can be unbounded once you have discovered how your lover best enjoys this particular pleasure.

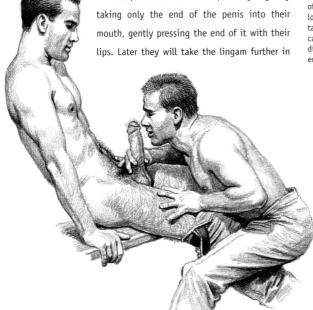

BELOW Worship of the lingam – so common in Indian philosophies – becomes literal for many gay men as they abase themselves at the altar of the phallus. Kneeling is a common position for fellatio.

and use their tongue and a sucking action to bring rapture to their lover, eventually taking in the whole shaft.

The fellator can then move his head back and forth over the shaft, continuing with the sucking and tongue movements until his lover either ejaculates or calls for an end to the pleasure. Alternatively, the man being fellated can thrust his penis within his lover's mouth, sometimes holding on to his head or hair to steady him for maximum purchase. This is called irrumation.

Fellatio is useful when sex is hurried and perhaps furtive – perhaps in some semi-public place where little preparation is possible and where no elaborate variations are feasible.

The veneration of the lingam is never better demonstrated than during oral sex, when elaborate rites of teasing and hard sucking can alternate. There are many possible variations on fellatio, which can be achieved in different postures. The organ can be brought to excitement by preliminary attention from the tongue on surrounding areas, so that the balls may be licked or gently sucked.

Positions for fellatio

WORSHIP OF THE LINGAM. In this position, the man being fellated stands, while his fellator kneels before him, taking the organ in his mouth. This has all the characteristics of a posture of worship and allows a lot of movement by the man in the kneeling position. Massaging the anus or penetrative fingering can accompany fellatio for extra pleasure. The man being fellated can also masturbate the exposed area of his cock while his lover sucks and licks the sensitive end parts. The fellator can, of course, masturbate himself as he works to pleasure his lover.

SIXTY-NINE. Mutual fellatio can be achieved in several positions, on the side and on top. On their sides, the two lovers lie with their bodies facing each other, from head to toe. They will then be able to please each other simultaneously. Alternatively, one can lie on his back, while the other kneels over him, head to toe. Another variation is for one man to sit in a high-backed armchair, while his lover suspends himself upside down in such a position that each can fellate the other. Strong arms are required for this. For the truly acrobatic, sixty-nine can be achieved standing up, with the standing lover holding his partner round the waist, upside down.

Because the penis always goes into the mouth 'upside down' when sixty-nining – with the sensitive part of the glans on the roof of the mouth – it is difficult to give this the same attention with the tongue as in one-at-a-time oral sex. Despite this small disadvantage, mutual fellatio remains extremely popular.

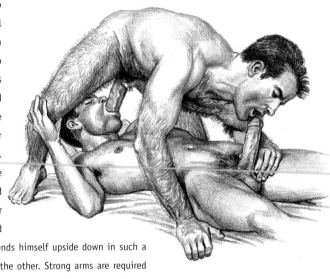

BELOW Sixty-nining – or mutual fallatio – can be enjoyed in a variety of positions and is very popular among gay men. There is something very satisfying and exciting in knowing that you and your lover are being equally pleasured, simultaneously.

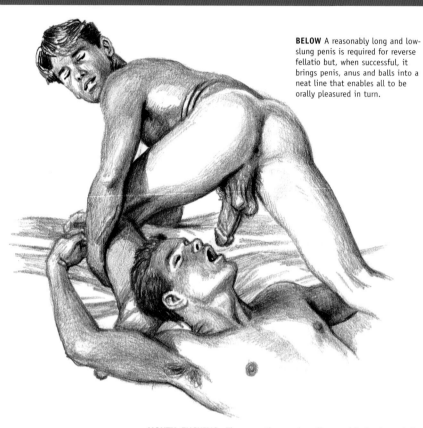

BELOW A reasonably long and low-slung penis is required for reverse fellatio but, when successful, it brings penis, anus and balls into a neat line that enables all to be orally pleasured in turn.

MOUTH FUCKING The receptive partner lies on his back, and the active partner straddles his shoulders, offering his penis for attention. He may lean over so that the penis can be taken in by his partner's eager mouth. The partner on top can stretch out his legs, raise himself up and thrust. This can also be done the other way around, with the receptive lover lying on his back on a bed, with his head hanging over the edge. His partner can then approach from the head end and insert his penis into his lover's mouth and begin thrusting.

REVERSE FELLATIO. The lover to be fellated gets down on all fours at the edge of the bed or couch with legs well apart, thrusting out his buttocks to expose all sensitive regions. His lover approaches from behind, grasps the penis and pulls it backwards between the legs. It can then be fellated from behind, with alternative attention being paid to the balls and anus, which will be well exposed.

The lingam can be anointed with delicious foods such as cream, honey, chocolate sauce and preserves for a sensual repast eaten from the organ of your loved one.

Fellatio can become the central act for many gay men, but some practice is needed to become skilled in the art. Beginners sometimes find that if the penis is long and goes too far down the throat, it can make them gag. More experienced lovers will have mastered this reaction and will be able to accommodate even the longest penis.

BELOW When a lover is enjoying oral attention from his partner he can further excite both of them by using his hands to stimulate the various erogenous zones that are within reach.

ABOVE Licking and teasing the penis with the tongue provides a pleasant and exciting interlude in an otherwise frantic sexual episode. Take time to explore and taste fully. Some men with a large penis have a wide opening on the end, and sometimes it is pleasant to explore this with the end of the tongue.

Sharp or broken teeth can also pose a problem for the inexperienced. Always be aware of the sensitivity of the skin on the shaft of the penis, and be careful not to allow your teeth to scrape on it.

Those who particularly enjoy giving fellatio will know the problems of an extended session. The muscles around the jaws can become stiff and aching, and so it is important to take a rest from time to time.

Recent research shows that fellatio is a very poor transmitter of HIV, and researchers have been unable to identify a single case of infection that was caused by oral sex. Rules on swallowing semen can therefore be relaxed. It is purely a matter of personal preference as to whether you like your partner to ejaculate in your mouth, or whether you would prefer him to withdraw. Ask him to indicate when he is going to come, and you can then make your decision.

Although HIV may not be the problem for fellators that it was once feared, other sexually transmitted diseases are. We will look more closely at these later.

Anal intercourse

The techniques for relaxing the anus so that fingers can be inserted comfortably can also be applied to the ultimate expression of male love – anal intercourse. Before considering the various positions that can be employed, we need to look at how intercourse can be made more comfortable for the receptive partner.

As with the insertion of fingers, it is important that the sphincter muscle that surrounds the anus is sufficiently relaxed that it avoids pain upon penetration. Some lovers prepare their partner for penetration by spending some time dilating the anus with the fingers and sometimes with small dildos (perhaps increasing in size as relaxation increases). Always use a lot of lubrication during this process so that entry can be achieved with the minimum of force. Condoms should be worn at all times unless you are absolutely sure of your health status and that of your partner.

Once the anus is sufficiently relaxed, the insertor should carefully rub the end of his erect penis over the anus, probing gently and pushing slightly harder to see if it will slip in easily. If there is resistance, continue to massage the anus with the fingers, inserting them again. Your partner will, at the same time, be consciously attempting to relax his sphincter. Make another attempt to insert the lingam, gently pushing at the anus until it penetrates. Be sensitive to your partner's reactions, and if he shows pain, ask if he would like you to withdraw. If he says 'yes', pull out gently, and wait a few moments, perhaps kissing your lover and gently massaging the anus with your fingers, reassuring him that all will be well.

BELOW This vessel, showing two men having sex, originated in the Chimu culture of northern Peru and dates from the fifteenth century. The Chimu culture was eventually overwhelmed by the Incas in 1460.

Now make another attempt, applying even more lubricant to the outside and inside of the anus with your fingers. Your partner may want to try to guide your penis to the right spot and assist with your efforts to enter him.

Once you have penetrated your partner, and he is comfortable, you can begin your thrusts. Start slowly, being aware at all times of your partner's reactions. It may take a few moments for him to accustom himself to the sensations he is feeling, and to find that they are pleasurable.

When you are ready, and he assents, you can start to thrust more forcefully and at greater speed. Once this is achieved, you can then experiment with different positions, different methods of thrusting and gyrating the hips, and other ways of gaining pleasure.

Some men find it possible to maintain an erection quite easily while being anally fucked, while others find it virtually impossible. The overwhelming sensations from the anus require full and complete attention, and the erection simply disappears. This should not be taken as a sign that he is not enjoying the experience; often it means the reverse.

Positions for anal intercourse

There are basically four positions for gay intercourse; these are standing, kneeling, sitting and lying down. There are many variations on these four basic themes.

A couple's favoured positions will depend very much on their compatibility in height and weight. Where a position requires a fairly well-matched height, cushions, chairs, stools, tables of various heights and even stepladders can help. But there are limits, and height differences can render some positions virtually impossible.

Standing

The standing positions are pleasurable and comfortable and give both partners a full opportunity for erotic involvement. Some are rather athletic and require practice, suppleness and strength.

Two Pillars. Here, the active partner approaches his lover from behind and penetrates him while standing. If lovers are of different heights, then it may be possible to compensate by the shorter lover standing on a step or a large book. It is difficult for the lovers to kiss in this position, although it does permit the man who is being penetrated to stimulate himself or, alternatively, for his partner to reach around and masturbate him as he thrusts.

Willows bent in the breeze. The receptive partner bends over, perhaps supported by a chair, table or bed, while his lover approaches from behind and penetrates him. The active lover can then lean over his partner and grasp something (the headboard, perhaps, or a doorknob) that will allow him harder, deeper thrusts. He can also reach around and stimulate his lover's lingam or nipples.

Kissing is difficult in this position, although ear nibbling and neck kissing are possible.

The pillar and the ivy. In this position, the lovers face each other. The one who is to be penetrated wraps his legs around his partner's waist, while holding fast around his neck. The partner who is to penetrate can also offer support for his lover's back and buttocks.

It will obviously be easier if the one to be suspended is smaller and lighter than the one who will stand and support him. It requires strength and an element of determination to sustain this position for very long, but it is an attractive novelty to try from time to time.

Squat. The receptive partner stands on the edge of a table, facing backwards, and then squats down, balancing himself by embracing his knees. This opens the buttocks and permits the active partner to approach from a standing-on-the-floor position and achieve penetration. This, too, requires some practice, and needs a table of precisely the right height.

Kneeling

The dog. In this, probably the most popular position, the one who is to be penetrated kneels on all fours and his partner approaches from behind, also on all fours. It offers great manoeuvrability, and

BELOW The doggy is probably the most commonly employed sexual position for anal intercourse among gay men. It allows the active partner a full range of movement, including thrusting and grinding.

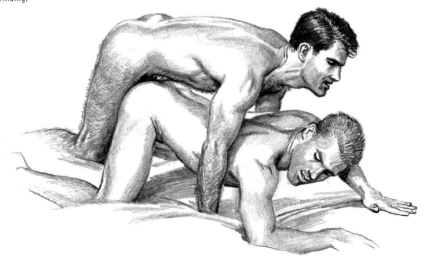

the active lover can easily vary the depth and speed of his thrusts, performing rotating movements with his hips for extra excitement. Kissing is difficult in this position, but many other variations are possible to give slightly different sensations. The active partner, for instance, can squat on his haunches rather than kneel, which allows for a different angle of thrust. He can drape himself over his partner's back and amuse himself by reaching around and playing with his partner's lingam and nipples.

BELOW The butterfly position is not easily achieved – nor is it sustainable for long periods. The advantage is that it allows both partners some control over movement and penetration.

The butterfly. In the butterfly position, the active partner kneels and thrusts his loins forward while supporting himself with his arms behind him. His partner then straddles him in a similar position, supporting himself in the same way, and then impales himself upon his lover's waiting lingam. In this position, the partner who is penetrated is able to control the speed, depth and direction of the strokes. The lover who has penetrated can also take some control by grasping his partner's hips and buttocks and moving him up and down to the rhythm of his own desires.

Sitting

In the sitting position its possible to enjoy many variations on the theme. Employing different locations and items of furniture – bed, chairs, floor – provides the opportunity for a wide variety of sensations to be experienced. For instance, the penetrator can sit on a chair without arms and his lover can sit astride him, supporting himself with his feet or toes upon the floor. This can be varied with the use of an armchair, when the lover to be penetrated positions his feet on the arms and lowers himself on to his partner's erect penis. In this position, the man underneath can, to some extent, do the thrusting, but in most cases, it is the man on top who controls the action. In this case, the distinction between the 'active' and the 'passive' partner becomes blurred.

The same effect can be achieved on the floor or on a bed, where the man to be penetrated straddles the loins of his lover, who is lying on his back. He then sits upon the lingam, and is once again in control of the strength and speed of thrusts. The penetrator can also position his buttocks on a small stool and drape himself so that he is supported on the floor by his head and his feet. This thrusts his hips forward and displays the lingam in its greatest magnificence. It also gives his lover more purchase with which to control the strokes.

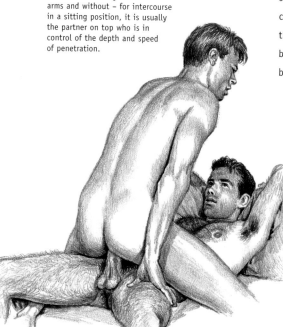

BELOW When using chairs – with arms and without – for intercourse in a sitting position, it is usually the partner on top who is in control of the depth and speed of penetration.

BELOW Another sitting position, this time on a harder surface, which has less 'give' and can therefore help in controlling the depth of penetration.

Lying down

Clasping. This involves the passive lover lying on his stomach, perhaps supported in the loins by pillows so that his buttocks are raised. His lover drapes himself over him and penetration is achieved. This allows much room for variation, and changes of tempo, although the man underneath may find stimulation of his organ difficult if it is encased in pillows

BELOW With the passive lover lying flat on his stomach, it is difficult for him to pleasure himself as his partner penetrates him. But this position is comfortable and easy to sustain for long periods

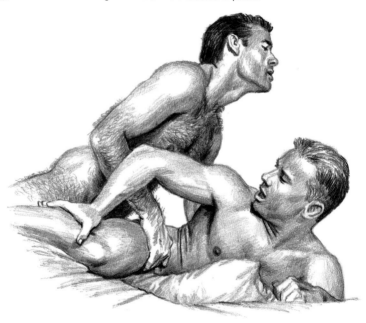

Sideways. The lovers lie close together on their sides, facing in the same direction. The lover behind, who is to penetrate, lifts his partner's leg, revealing and opening the anus. He then gains penetration. It is easy to bring his lover to climax by massaging his lingam at the same time.

Sitting on top. The penetrator lies on his back, while the one to be penetrated straddles his loins with his knees bent. He can do this facing his lover, or facing away. If he faces his lover, he can lean over and kiss him. If he faces away, his lover gets a better view of the penetration, which is exciting for some men.

The crab. This is a difficult one, mainly practised by those with more experience – and strong arms. The penetrator lies on his back, and his lover lies on top of him, face up. Penetration is achieved in this position, and then the lovers simultaneously raise themselves from the ground on arms and legs, maintaining the penetration. The active lover can then thrust, although it is difficult to gain much purchase in this position, and it is difficult to maintain for more than a few seconds at a time. The advantage is that in this posture, the prostate can be stimulated more effectively.

BELOW Lying on their sides, the lovers can kiss and lick each other's face and neck during intercourse. Thrusting is easy, and new sensations can be created with a little imagination.

Yawning. The man to be penetrated lies on his back and places a cushion beneath himself, just above his buttocks. He pulls his legs well apart and bends his knees, thrusting his buttocks forward. His partner can then penetrate easily. This position allows kissing and the massage of the passive partner's organ. From this initial position, many other variations are possible. The active lover can keep pushing the passive partner upwards, until he is almost resting on his shoulders.

The Trapeze. The receptive partner lies on his back on the floor and pulls his legs over his shoulders so that his anus is exposed. The active partner puts a chair or low table behind him and suspends himself over his partner, with his feet on the chair, and his arms supporting him on the floor. He enters his partner and proceeds to thrust. This is a position for more experienced lovers, and the active partner needs strong arms.

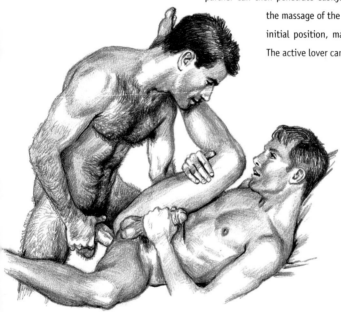

ABOVE In this position, the lovers face each other and can kiss. The passive partner can raise his legs higher and higher until eventually he is almost resting on his shoulders, at which point it almost becomes a different position in which the active partner can penetrate from varying angles.

Other novelties

DOUBLE RUB. The naked lovers stand close, facing each other, leaning back slightly from the waist and thrusting their loins together. One of the lovers takes both penises in one hand and stimulates them together by rubbing and moving his hand up and down in a masturbatory movement. Lubrication can increase the pleasure.

PYJAMA GAMES. Buy the largest pair of pyjamas or jogging pants you can find. Both participants then get into the pyjama bottoms, either facing each other or back to front. They then attempt to have sex either by rubbing or by anal penetration.

THE TRAIN. (Also called daisy chain.) Any number, from three upwards, can participate in this. The first man fucks the second man, while the third man fucks the second and so on. This can be achieved in a number of positions.

Dog fashion. This probably has a maximum of three participants, as it becomes difficult to fold any more over each other. Also, co-ordinating thrusts can be difficult.

Standing. This is probably best for larger groups. The participants simply enter each other from behind in a chain. Difficult to sustain as group co-ordination is required to keep it going.

The missionary's dog. The first man lies on his back with his legs pulled back. The second man enters him in the yawning position. The third man enters the second man from behind, in the dog position.

ABOVE This Indian miniature depicts two homosexual couples having sex. It shows that homosexuality was not, as some later scholars have claimed, a rare occurrence in India.

Group sex

When more than two men get together for a sexual experience there are added pleasures and added dangers. The number of possible combinations and positions increases exponentially according to the number of participants, but so do the possibilities of emotional problems. Established partners can successfully introduce a third party into their lovemaking as a means of spicing it up, but if one of the partners should find that the other two are more interested in sex with each other than with three, he can feel jealous and excluded. It can also cause damage to the original relationship.

But if all partners are willing and happy with the situation, and feel equally involved, then much pleasure can be derived from the possible permutations. Perhaps the most popular three-way position is for one man to bend over and be entered from the rear while at the same time fellating a third person. This basic position can be varied in all the ways described for couples – sitting, standing, lying down.

Four lips is a variation for three people. One stands while the other two kneel at either side of him, facing each other. The two men in the kneeling position then kiss, with the other man's penis between their four lips. He can then thrust, or they can move their heads up and down the shaft in unison. In effect he is having a double blow-job.

In the roundelay, the participants lie down in a circle and fellate each other simultaneously. Any number of men can participate in such a circle.

One man can fellate while the other performs anilingus, one can fuck one of the partners, while the third can offer either of them his penis to be fellated. Two partners can sixty-nine in the lying position, while the third fucks the one on top.

All of the methods of sexual congress can be deployed and extended for three, with each of them taking it in turn to be the centre of attention.

BELOW In a group sex situation, a complete circle is achieved so that all participants can orally please each other. The positioning in the circle can be changed from time to time so that everyone has a turn with everyone else.

Relationships

Gay relationships can extend over many decades or they may last only one night. Whether long or short term, they should be treated with respect, and the participants should aim not only to pleasure each other's bodies but to enhance each other's minds and spirits. When you share something of yourself with another person, it should enrich you both, and when you offer your bodies to each other, it should involve more than just the ambition to achieve an orgasm.

It would be unrealistic to expect every sexual encounter to be a transcendental, life-changing experience. Sometimes there is no empathy, no connection, no common ground between you and your partner, and you both accept that you do not want to pursue the connection. But even when this happens, it should not mean that you cannot treat your sexual partners with the dignity they deserve as human beings. A kind word about some aspect of them that is worthy of a compliment will send them away feeling that they have not been used, or that your uniting was not a dishonourable thing.

It ennobles us to be generous in our acceptance that, although we tried to connect, we failed. We may not have been right for one another, but that does not make us worthless as people. Let us part on good terms, even if we do not intend to see each other again.

When the spark of mutual passion does strike, however, it can be wonderful. What started out as a no-questions-asked sexual encounter can end up transforming your life, giving you a loving companion who will share your highs and lows, your dreams and secrets. It can give you instant access to sexual satisfaction and allow you to explore the deeper levels of erotic experience. Having sex with someone you love is a qualitatively different experience from sex with a stranger whom you will probably never see again.

Developing relationships

Like all relationships that extend over a long period, gay partnerships change and evolve as the years pass, but the changes can be so gradual that partners may not realize they are happening, and misunderstandings can sometimes arise.

Partners do not always pass from one stage of development of their relationship to the next at the same time, and so changes can be misinterpreted as a loss of interest. If, for instance, one partner is still in the passionate 'honeymoon' period of the relationship, craving sex at all times of night and day, while his partner has moved on to the less frantic second period, where the emphasis is placed on home making, then there may be a mistaken perception that the relationship has run its course.

LEFT In this Greek vase painting, from the fifth century BCE, two young men are seen washing and grooming each other, using the relaxed occasion maybe for a little erotic pleasure.

ABOVE This depiction of the legendary battle between Hercules and Antaeus is suffused with homoeroticism. When Hercules realized that Antaeus was gaining his apparent invincibility from the earth, he held him off the ground until his strength drained away.

Couples need to accept that their relationship will evolve – although maybe not entirely in synchronization. This should prepare them to realize that their partner's changing priorities are probably not a sign that it's all over. It's just becoming different. And each stage of an extended relationship has its own consolations and pleasures.

If a couple have decided that they want to make a serious commitment to each other, they should be aware of, and have prepared for, the changes that will inevitably overtake them, and sometimes perplex them. If they can get through these changes together, their partnership will endure.

Research into gay relationships shows that the initial period of mad passion, in which sexual activity plays a dominant role, transforms itself into the next phase, which has been called 'nesting'. The emphasis then shifts to creating a secure and comfortable environment in which the couple can flourish. Companionship overtakes sex as the most important element. As the couple becomes accepted and acknowledged by their friends and family, their love will deepen, but their sexual interest may die.

Familiarity can breed contempt if you let it, and an unchanging routine can create boredom. Unless this is recognized, it is easy to fall into a comfortable, but sexless, partnership. This suits some couples, whose love deepens and becomes stronger with the passing years, but whose sexual passion dims.

Sustaining sexual interest over a longer period, though, requires application. Unless you work at it, and constantly tell your partner that you still find him attractive, and that you still have new avenues of eroticism to explore, you can descend into destructive routines of indifference and boredom. It is at this stage that you may begin to look for new erotic adventures outside your relationship. After several years together, gay couples will often accept that, although they love each other and feel that their commitment is for life, their sexual outlet may need to be found elsewhere.

There are obvious dangers in this, such as jealousy and the possibility that one of your casual lovers will turn out to be more appealing than your present partner.

Some researchers have shown that gay couples who have been together for 20 years or more will often begin to rekindle their sexual interest in each other. In such circumstances – and earlier in the relationship, too – the use of Tantra, or ritualized sexual encounters, can help. Tantra says that loving your partner in a sexual way does not always have to be centred on the genitals. Sex should be a whole body and mind experience that helps couples grow closer and more loving. The desire to respect and cherish those we love, as well as to make love to them, can be expressed and developed effectively through Tantra.

Lovers of long standing may need to revisit their early passion, reminiscing and trying to recreate the profound desire that once sparked between them.

BELOW However long a gay relationship may have lasted, it can still provide sexual pleasure and loving moments for partners. Though the underlying love may be deep, it can take effort and commitment to keep the flame of desire alive.

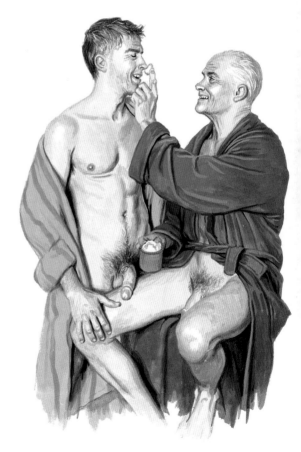

Those who are serious about reviving their physical as well as their emotional attachment might like to read a few books about the philosophy of Tantric sex, or seek out a practitioner who can help them explore it more deeply.

In order to sustain our relationships, perhaps in the face of disapproval and pressure from those around us, we must learn to be strong and proud, and to be absolutely convinced of the value of our love. If we come to accept other people's disapproval of our gayness, then we are in trouble. The more secretive we are about our relationship, the more difficult it is to make it successful. If we are required to deny that our love exists, then our relationship is immediately debased. That is why we must let those we love know that we are a couple, and that we need them to recognize the importance we attach to the life we have with our partner.

Communication is another essential skill for a successful relationship. You must strive to be honest and open with your partner, and not to play games with his emotions. Once again, a high level of self-esteem is important here. For unless we value our own feelings and those of other people equally, we will find it difficult to say what we mean, to ask for what we want and even to say 'no' when it may be hurtful.

The *Kama Sutra* describes many styles of quarrel between lovers, but accepts that arguments are sometimes necessary in order to get hidden resentments and frustrations out in the open. Once it is clear that one partner is not happy with something, then the couple can, together, begin to find an answer to their problem. If it remains hidden and unsaid, such resentment can fester and become bitter, leading to stale, unhappy relationships characterized by constant sniping and a lack of real communication.

Communication is not always easy, but successful couples have found ways to make their feelings known and to navigate together the difficult areas of disagreement. And arguments, however hurtful and nasty, can end in a reconciliation that needs to be expressed sexually.

Vatsyayana tells of the special sex that can follow from a disagreement that has been rectified. The lovers are anxious to regain the loving feelings, and a special intimacy can develop at such times.

As we have said, older couples sometimes find that after many years together, the erotic flame that they thought had died suddenly reignites. They find a new interest, and begin to explore once more.

Sex for the older man must, of necessity, be slower and more considered. The body will not be as supple as it was in youth, and so the more acrobatic sex will no longer be an option. Nevertheless, many other options remain open. Lovemaking for older couples may be more sedate, but it need be no less passionate.

Sexual problems

Sex is not always perfect. Our bodies and our minds sometimes let us down, and bring anxiety into our love life. But if we are aware of the problems that can occur, we are less likely to be emotionally paralyzed by them.

Sexual stimulation sends a message to the brain, which responds by sending nerve signals to the penis. A chemical messenger is produced by the nerve endings that then causes the blood vessels in the penis to open up, resulting in an erection. Sometimes, though, something happens to interfere with this process, and the erection simply doesn't happen.

Failure to achieve or maintain an erection can be devastating for some men. Their self-esteem plummets, self-recrimination rages. They become anxious about intimacy, and may even start to avoid it. Embarrassment and feelings of humiliation stop some men seeking help, and they suffer in silence.

Most problems with getting an erection have a physical cause. These can include diabetes and arterial disease, alcoholism and the side effects of some prescription drugs. Your doctor can advise you about the best options in these cases.

Excessive anxiety about 'performing well' can also cause erection failure. After it has failed once, the anxiety rises even further and so, at the next attempt, there is another no-show and it becomes a self-perpetuating crisis. Counselling from a qualified sex therapist can help in such cases. Tantric sex, which can take the focus away from the genitals and from the need to 'perform' in a particular way, has also been very useful to men who are having problems with erections.

Many men have found the drug Viagra helpful, too. Your doctor can give you a prescription for this. During the time that Viagra stays in your system, it will help you gain and maintain an erection. Viagra has been shown to help up to 80 per cent of those with symptoms of erectile dysfunction. There are also surgical treatments and suction devices that can be tried, although success rates vary. New generations of drugs are being developed that will have a longer-lasting effect than Viagra, and your physician can give you advice about these.

A cock ring can help maintain an erection. This is a device – normally made of metal or leather – that is pushed over the prick, and sometimes the balls, to restrict the flow of blood back down the penis. Actors often use them in porn movies to sustain an erection for many hours. They are safe when used in moderation. You can buy them from sex shops, on the Internet or by mail order.

Men for whom impotence is a problem should not hesitate to consult a urologist or sex therapist. There is no need for embarrassment – the consultant will have seen these problems in many, many other men and will treat them matter of factly.

There is no need to panic if you find that you 'come too soon'. Premature ejaculation is one of the most common sexual problems in men and the one most likely to be self-correcting. If it persists, however, there are effective ways of training yourself to slow down. You can practise this method when masturbating: as soon as you feel the orgasm approaching (but before it becomes inevitable), squeeze the end of your penis between your thumb and forefinger quite hard. This will cause the rush towards orgasm to stop and maybe some of the erection to be lost. After the sensation has passed, repeat the process as many times as you can manage without coming. This will have the effect of training your body not to over-react to sexual stimulation.

Once again, the study and practice of Tantric sex can be helpful in assuring you that orgasm need not be the one and only aim of your sexual encounters. And, should your partner find himself experiencing any of these difficulties, you can help by being gentle, patient and reassuring.

ABOVE The cock ring is an ancient device that still proves its worth in helping maintain an erection over a long period. It restricts the flow of blood out of the penis and so helps keep it firm. It is safe to use so long as it is not too tight and does not cut into the flesh.

Chapter 4:
On the knowledge
that lovers need

health and beautification

ABOVE With modern medicine, we can now obtain relief and protection from the diseases associated with love. But where medicine cannot cure, knowledge and safer sex is by far the best protection.

OPPOSITE Perseus was a Greek god of great beauty, bravery and daring, an early archetype for many modern Hollywood heroes known to attract a large gay following. One of his greatest adventures, depicted here, was the rescuing of Andromeda from the jaws of a sea monster.

Knowledge of the ailments that can accompany sexual activity is essential. Then emphasis can be placed on beautifying and perfuming your body in ways that will help you attract lovers.

Sexually transmitted diseases

HIV is transmitted through blood and other bodily fluids. The most common way in which it passes between gay men is through unprotected anal intercourse. The only known protection is condoms and safer sex. Once the virus has been acquired, there is no cure. Practise safer sex at all times, and the likelihood is that you will live a long and happy life, full of sexual excitement and variety.

Hepatitis B and C are blood-borne viruses that attack the liver. They spread in much the same way as HIV, but are a hundred times more infectious; a very large percentage of active gay men are already infected. Some kinds of hepatitis are potentially life threatening.

Symptoms of hepatitis include tiredness, nausea, lack of appetite and aversion to drinking alcohol and smoking. During the acute stage of the illness, when it is at its most infectious, the sufferer's skin may become yellow and he might have a fever, dark urine, pale stools and abdominal tenderness in the area of the liver.

ABOVE The rigid separation of men from women in some cultures has encouraged the formation of homosexual subcultures. In this picture a Persian king is entertained by his page.

Recovery takes up to six months, during which time the sufferer is lethargic and depressed. However, there may be no symptoms at all, or they might be so mild as to go unnoticed.

Once acquired, there is no cure for hepatitis, but there is a vaccine that offers protection in the majority of cases. If you are a sexually active gay man, it is wise to go to your doctor and ask for the vaccination.

Genital herpes, caused by the herpes simplex virus, can be very painful. It is the same virus that causes cold sores, and similar eruptions can appear anywhere on the body. Gay men who have had sex with someone with a herpes infection are likely to find signs of the infection on their penis or anus. There is no cure yet, but ointments can speed up the eradication of blisters. If you are infected, do not have sex while the blisters are on your body, as they are highly infectious; you should also watch out for them on your lover's body. It is safe to have sex when the blisters are not present.

Syphilis, one of the most dangerous venereal diseases, can remain undetected because the symptoms vary so widely and aren't always recognized. In its final stage it can cripple, or even kill, its victims.

Syphilis is usually passed on by sexual contact. Contrary to common misconceptions, you can't get it from drinking from a glass or from contact with a toilet seat or door handle. The bacteria that cause syphilis tend to thrive in the moist, warm areas of the body, so they can enter through the genitals, the throat, the anus or the mouth. The first sign of syphilis is a sore, which is about the size of a baked bean and shows itself about four weeks after infection. If it is in a concealed place, you might not even notice it.

The next phase sometimes manifests itself as a rash and, possibly, a fever. Within two weeks, the second phase will have passed and the bacteria will go into hiding in your body. It might remain inactive but it could reappear for the third, or tertiary stage, when it might attack the heart or the nervous system. Syphilis can be treated with antibiotics if caught in the earlier stages. It is essential to arrange regular check-ups if you are a sexually active man.

Gonorrhoea is the commonest of the STDs and is rampant in the gay community. It can be treated quickly and easily with antibiotics. If you think you might have caught a dose, see your doctor as soon as possible – and, in the meantime, abstain from sex.

Gonorrhoea enters the body through the mucous membranes, so you might get infected through your mouth, throat, rectum or eyes. Probably the first indication that you have contracted it will be a discharge of pus from your penis. You might notice it on your pyjamas or underpants. Sometimes there are no symptoms, and you'll be unaware that you have the disease. But left untreated it can lead to a form of arthritis. While you are sexually active, you should get yourself checked out regularly.

Pubic lice, sometimes called crabs, are troublesome creatures that can be passed during sexual contact. They live and breed in the pubic hair, feeding on the blood, causing itching and irritation. They can be eradicated with special treatments, readily available from pharmacies. Don't try to treat them by spraying yourself with insecticide – it could prove dangerous.

Beautifying and perfuming the body

One of the common stereotypes of gay men is that they are all beautifully toned, fashionably dressed, expensively coiffed and oozing good taste. Certainly there are many gay men, particularly the ones who are competing in the market for sex and romance, who take extremely good care of themselves.

While not everyone wants to spend large amounts of time in the gym, or has the money to buy expensive designer clothes, there is still plenty that you can do to make yourself more attractive. Indeed, some of the more desirable males we see around us are far from expensively dressed – sometimes worn and tattered clothing give erotic emphasis to a good build.

We have said that the *Kama Sutra* encourages the cultivation of many life skills so that we will not have to depend exclusively on our youth and physical beauty to be attractive to others. There is no shortage of readily available grooming aids for men, and books and magazines on looking good, keeping fit and dressing well proliferate on the news-stands. Read some of these and see what the experts have to say. Most of all, though, choose the style that makes you feel most comfortable.

The image you choose to adopt will rest entirely with how confident you feel with it, and what you can afford. If you are thinking of making changes in the way you present yourself, ask for the opinion of friends that you trust. Experiment and give yourself frequent make-overs until you find what works best for you in the arena of romantic liaisons.

Even if you do not have film star looks or a gym-toned body, you can still have a beautifully modulated voice that speaks of dark secrets and erotic potential. You can show an interest in other

OPPOSITE With no soap available, this well-proportioned athlete from the fifth century is using the traditional method of cleansing – he pours olive oil over his body and then scrapes it off with a strigil, an implement usually made from wood or metal.

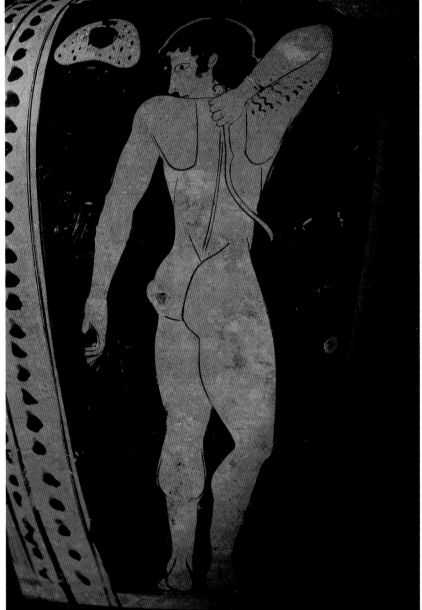

people's lives and activities, and be able to share what your lover loves enthusiastically, and this will bring happiness and the interest of others.

The *Kama Sutra* teaches that there is a very powerful connection between the sense of smell, sexual excitement and fulfilment. Lovers should bathe and scent themselves with essences of flowers, perfumes and scented oils before engaging in intimate encounters. The burning of incense and the rubbing in of sandalwood ointments is also recommended.

Modern selections of soaps and body oils for men, as well as pre-shave and after-shave lotions, are almost endless. In the days of Vatsyayana, perfumes and unguents were precious commodities, reserved exclusively for the very rich and privileged classes. Now, enticing and exotic perfumes are available to everyone and, with careful selection, they can create an association in your lover's mind between you, your perfume and sexual experience.

Cleanliness is, of course, one of the prime virtues for lovers. And showering or bathing together can be a wonderful experience. Vatsyayana does not encourage sexual play in water, regarding semen as precious and not something that should come into contact with water. Earlier scholars, though, found that sexual experience using water was delightful and to be enjoyed.

Sex in the shower or jacuzzi is a common fantasy in gay pornography, and the pleasures are widely copied. The slap of water on the skin during sex creates a strange and pleasant sensation. The shower head can, of course, be detached and the jet of hard, warm water aimed at sensitive parts of the body, such as the anus and the penis, to produce a marvellous sensation. Power showers come into their own in this scenario.

OPPOSITE Though earlier scholars advocated water play for lovers, Vatsyayana disapproved of it because it destroyed 'divine' semen. Modern showers, baths, swimming pools and hot-tubs present plenty of opportunities for submerged sex.

If your bathtub is big enough for two, then many happy hours can be devoted to luxuriating in perfumed water. The hot-tub and the sauna also have their aficionados and because of their association with nudity, they have become eroticized.

Bathing each other as a prelude to sex is an experience that many find profoundly appealing. Decorate the bathroom with scented candles, and rub perfumed oils into the skin of your loved one. Washing the private areas of your lover has an intimacy that serves as a perfect overture to love.

Body hair

The question of body hair is one that exercises many gay men. Having spent a great deal of time and effort toning their physique, many are reluctant to have the resulting contours hidden by hair. The use of depilatory creams and waxing are two methods of removing body hair, and wet-shaving the body has been made into an erotic experience in its own right.

Some men like to shave just the hair on their chest, so that their hard-won, clearly defined pectoral muscles can be viewed without the line being broken. Others prefer to shave their whole body – even their head – to present a smooth and glistening expanse of flesh to their lover.

If you have decided to shave your body, why not make it into an exciting sexual experience by inviting your lover to do it for you? After shaving your chest, you might invite him to cut and shave the hair in your more intimate regions. The pubic hair can be shaped into interesting designs, while shaving the buttocks on the outside and between the crack can be a marvellous turn-on.

For extra excitement, dry the area well and then finish off by shaving around the anus with an electric razor.

Removing hair from around the anus makes it easier and more hygienic to use as a sexual playground, although, of course, there can be irritation and itching when the hair begins to grow back. Soothing creams can be purchased from the pharmacy to overcome this inconvenience.

Increasingly, however, body hair is regarded as an erotic indication of masculinity, and more men are opting for shaping and tidying rather than complete removal.

LEFT This detail from a mosaic found in Tunisia shows the smooth-skinned shepherd boy Endymion catching the eye of the goddess Selene. The removal of male body hair for reasons of hygiene, aestheticism and eroticism has been practised in various cultures for centuries. However, hirsuteness is increasingly seen as a badge of vigorous masculinity.

Tattoos

Tattooing is an ancient art found in most cultures, and its appeal is timeless. The special inks and dyes used for tattoos are injected under the skin surface and permanently trapped there by collagen. The process is achieved with needles driven by something like a sewing machine that punctures the skin at three thousand jabs a minute.

Tattooing is a specialized art, and not one to be attempted by amateurs. If you are contemplating having a tattoo, ensure that you go to a reputable artist who looks after his equipment and sterilizes his needles adequately. Unsterilized needles can result in the spread of HIV, hepatitis B and other blood-borne diseases.

Some people find the pain of having a tattoo applied a challenge that excites them, while others prefer the use of analgesic creams to help them through the process.

Some tattoos are small and discreetly placed, while others are large, covering huge areas of skin on the back or chest. But remember, once they have been applied, they are almost impossible to remove without a great deal of pain, expense and scarring. Think particularly hard before having tattoos applied to your face or any other exposed area.

If you are seriously considering having a tattoo, why not try a temporary version first, to see how you like it – and gauge how your lovers may react to it? The advantage of a temporary tattoo, either a transfer or a *mehndi*, is that when you're tired of it, you can change it for something else.

Transfers are an excellent choice for a single event, when you want to send out a particular message, and a quick search on the Internet will reveal a huge range of available transfers – both as small designs, armbands and pictures that cover much larger areas.

They are relatively cheap and easy to apply, and you can have a different tattoo for every season, event and occasion. Some manufacturers will create transfers to your own requirements, so imagination is your only limit.

Mehndi is another option for creating temporary tattoo-like designs on the skin. It consists of drawing on the skin with a paste

ABOVE The ancient arts of piercing and tattooing are still extremely popular in Western culture. Henna body art, or *mehndi*, is an alternative for those who don't want a permanent tattoo.

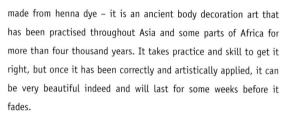

made from henna dye – it is an ancient body decoration art that has been practised throughout Asia and some parts of Africa for more than four thousand years. It takes practice and skill to get it right, but once it has been correctly and artistically applied, it can be very beautiful indeed and will last for some weeks before it fades.

Henna is produced from the leaves of a small shrub, *Lawsonia inermis*, which are dried and ground into a powder. This is then made into a paste and applied to the skin to create designs. Occasionally, henna can cause adverse skin reactions, so try a small concealed area first, especially if you are planning to apply it to large areas.

Mehndi kits are easily obtained from suppliers on the Internet or can be found in specialist body art shops. Traditional designs can be intricate, but you may want to create something more personal. You and your lover can spend time decorating the most intimate areas as part of your love play.

Piercing

Body piercing and the insertion of jewellery into the resulting holes is also an ancient art that has become popular once more. The whole ritual of body piercing has become complex and elaborate, and makes a strong statement about who you are and where you fit into society.

We are all familiar with ear piercing and ear-rings, but jewellery can also be inserted through the lips, the tongue, eyebrow, cheek and nose. Nipple-rings are also popular and navel piercing is common.

Piercing the genitals for decoration with various metal bars and jewels is popular with real fans of body art, but this can be dangerous, and must be undertaken with the greatest caution,

under the supervision of experienced and responsible operators.

These are the styles of genital piercing most common among men:

THE PRINCE ALBERT. This is probably the most popular of all male genital piercings. It is, in most cases, achieved by inserting a needle-receiving tube into the urethra and then introducing the needle from the outside and feeding it out through the tube. A metal ring is then inserted that goes into the urethra and comes out underneath or on top of the penis.

THE FRENUM. This very popular male piercing comes second only to the Prince Albert. The needle pierces the flexible skin of the underside of the shaft just behind the glans. There are two other

ABOVE This Greek amphora depicts a symposium. Symposia were drinking parties for men only. These events were often used by aristocrats as opportunities to instruct their younger lovers in the art of good citizenship – and sex.

variations of the frenum piercing: the lorum (lower frenum, placed at the base of the shaft near the scrotum) and the ladder (several frenum piercings from the base of the shaft to the top).

Foreskin piercing is obviously limited to the uncircumcised penis. Unlike ancient times when this was used as a chastity device for slaves, today it is used for sexual enhancement. The foreskin can be pierced with either single or multiple piercings.

The scrotum can be pierced just about anywhere and is relatively painless due to the thin elasticity of the skin. The disadvantages are that because of natural perspiration, and lack of ventilation, irritation is common, making the healing process difficult.

THE AMPALLANG. One of the more difficult male piercings, the ampallang is painful and can cause damage to the nerves and arteries in the penis if it is not done correctly. The hole is made horizontally through the glans, and this can be done above, under or through the urethra, depending on the individual. Because of the discomfort and potentially severe dangers, it is, unsurprisingly, not a popular choice.

THE APADRAVYA. This is similar to the Ampallang, except that instead of a horizontal piercing through the penis glans (head), it is a vertical piercing. It has been mentioned in the *Kama Sutra* as an erotic piercing for both visual and physical arousal. Once more, it can be a slow and extremely painful process, and can result in dangerous and prolonged bleeding if not done properly. The Apadravya is only for the most determined, to be carried out under strictly controlled conditions of hygiene.

These more esoteric piercings are, of course, the territory of experts. You should use only the most skilled, qualified and meticulously clean operators to undertake these enhancements, and you should be aware of the complications that can arise, seeking medical help immediately should anything go wrong.

Use only the best-quality jewellery from a reputable dealer in your piercings. Cheap jewellery can cause serious problems; toxic metals can leak into the urethra and cause damage to the kidneys.

The food of love

Aphrodisiacs – foods and chemicals that are reputed to stimulate sexual desire – are given a large section to themselves in the *Kama Sutra*. But few of the delicacies that Vatsyayana recommends are available to the average Western pleasure seeker. For instance, if a man wishes to 'become lovely in the eyes of others', he is enjoined to 'eat the powder of the *Melumbrium speciosum*, the blue lotus and

BELOW Dionysus was the Greek form of the God Bacchus, and is associated, among other things, with wine and wine making. His worshippers sometimes depicted him as a wild and unpredictable deity, released from inhibition by the consumption of wine.

the *Mesna roxburghil*, with ghee and honey.'

However, some of Vatsyayana's suggestions are for poisonous plants that would be downright dangerous to consume.

Several preparations are recommended for increasing sexual vigour. The easiest to prepare consists of equal parts of ghee (clarified butter), honey, sugar, liquorice, the juice of fennel bulbs and milk. This is described as 'a nectar-like composition' that provokes sexual vigour.

Milk, liquorice and sugar/honey play a central role in many of Vatsyayana's recipes. Additional ingredients can include a relative of the asparagus, shitawari (*Asparagus racemosus*), long pepper (*Piper longum*) and the seeds or roots of *Trapa bispinosa*.

More exotically, the *Kama Sutra* suggests boiling a ram's and a goat's testicle in milk, adding sugar, and drinking the concoction in order to increase the size of the penis. (Other recipes said to increase the size of the lingam by the application of various potions are, in the main, composed of poisonous substances that should be strictly avoided.)

Much more is known today about the effects of diet on the body than would have been possible in the days of Vatsyayana. Thanks to scientific advances, we now have very precise knowledge about what foods we must eat to keep the body strong, healthy, fit and lean, and those we must avoid if we are not to become flabby and lethargic. A diet that is rich in nutritious fruit and vegetables, nuts and seeds, with enough protein from meat or other sources to balance it, will ensure that your body is vigorous and capable of enjoying the sexual excitements that it craves. It will also help maintain strong hair and teeth and a youthful, complexion. Modern man will have to find his own foods of love, and keep to a diet that

OPPOSITE The search for aphrodisiacs – herbs and potions that stimulate sexual vigour – is common to all cultures throughout history. Now, pharmaceuticals routinely do the job that in ancient times was thought to need the intervention of magic.

is likely to increase his attractions to potential lovers.

The Roman citizen Seneca had this advice for his fellow countrymen who were searching obsessively for a magic concoction or ingredient that would increase libido and potency: 'I will show you a philtre without potions, without herbs, without any witch's incantation – if you wish to be loved, love.'

In many ways, the pharmaceutical industry has ended the search for aphrodisiacs with the introduction of Viagra and similar drugs. There is nothing magical about this pill – it is the product of science, and it works. Why fall for the blandishments of snake oil salesmen, when the answer lies with your own physician?

All the same, food can play a very important part in any romantic liaison, and because of this it can still be regarded as an essential element of a successful sexual encounter. Sharing a meal of special and exotic foods has always been a part of the ritual of courtship. Such a meal will engage all the senses and prepare the lovers to indulge themselves further. An artfully and carefully planned meal will stimulate smell, sight and taste. A glorious repast, shared in romantic surroundings, can lead to a state of euphoria that is very similar to a sexual experience.

Expensive and difficult-to-find ingredients that are unfamiliar will go some way to preparing the senses for other exotic and never-before-tasted delights to come later. Caviar (eggs of the sturgeon) and asparagus (notice the resemblance to the lingam) are favourites, as are truffles and other rare fungi. Champagne and other fine wines will lower inhibitions (although they are best taken in moderation, for, as Shakespeare says of alcohol, 'it provokes the desire, but it takes away the performance'). Finger foods are appropriate for the intimacy created by feeding

each other sweetmeats.

Seafood has a reputation for enhancing sexual desire. Oysters, lobsters, clams and mussels are often regarded as lovers' food, and fish such as sole and turbot will always impress (mainly because they are expensive). Chocolate, too, has been found to contain phenylethylamine, a substance that is also produced by the body when we are in love. Try to eat only the best quality chocolate with a high cocoa solid content (around 70 per cent is best).

If you are doubtful about your culinary skills, then a cosy, romantic restaurant is an easier option, but, wherever you dine, always make sure that the erotic meal is light, or you may find yourself becoming drowsy instead of horny.

ABOVE The story of Hercules and his legendary strength is an enduring myth that has inspired many a homoerotic fantasy. The appeal of the man-mountain is still as potent as ever, and heavily muscled actors are in great demand in gay erotica.

Massage

A sensual massage is the perfect prelude to an extended sexual episode, and fully exploits the sense of touch.

You can slowly and suggestively undress each other to begin with, gently brushing areas of skin as they are exposed.

When you are both naked, kneel facing each other and begin your massage with the head. Gently rub the temples in a circular motion, being careful not to apply too much pressure. Then move to the ears, caressing the lobes and gently running your finger

BELOW Undressing a lover can be slow and tantalizing, a wonderful prelude to artful lovemaking, or so urgent that it results in torn clothing. Either way, there can be endless pleasure and surprise in unpacking the goods.

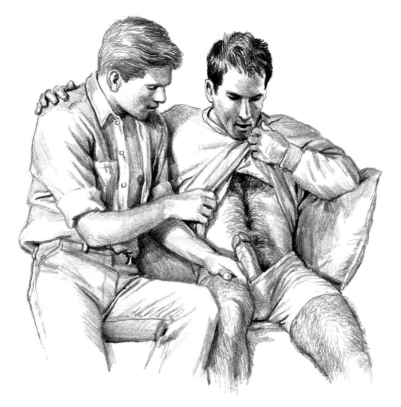

around the inside. Then tap your fingers in a symmetrical sweeping motion across the head, which helps release tension and create serenity. Tracing the shape of his nose, lips, cheeks and chin with your finger will show your partner how attractive you find him.

Now have your partner lie face down on a firm, but warm and comfortable surface, such as a rug. Straddle him and rest your hands on his upper back. Then apply pressure and stroke his back, shoulders, legs, hands and feet.

Give special attention to the hands and feet, stretching the fingers and toes and sucking and kissing them in anticipation of greater pleasures to come.

Stroke every part of your partner's body – nape of neck, armpits, back of knees, elbows and thighs. The buttocks need special attention as they contain firmer muscle and need to be pressed and kneaded harder. Push his legs apart and gently stroke the inner thigh, 'accidentally' brushing against his balls and anus to create erotic tension that can be released later.

Now turn your partner over and straddle him again. In order to increase his anticipation, you may not wish to make contact with his genitals yet, even though he may have an erection, so you can kneel beside him and start your massage at his shoulders. Sweep your hand down his chest in circular movements, paying particular attention to the nipples, which should be teased before working down to the abdomen. Use slightly firmer strokes to avoid tickling. Pay attention to the navel, and then rub both hips at once in a thrusting motion.

Brush provocatively past the genitals, making only the gentlest of contact as you by-pass them, to massage the legs and on down to the feet.

You can now add a more overtly sexual element to the massage, by licking and kissing and gently nibbling strategic areas. Start by caressing the neck with your lips. Then, nuzzle, kiss and lick the throat and chin and move on to the ears, which you can explore with your tongue. Move on to the nipples, which you should lick and suck and gently nibble.

BELOW Massage is an excellent way to relax your lover and build trust between you. Your manipulations are not only pleasant in their own right, they can become an important prelude to lovemaking.

Having created great expectations for your partner, you can gently move into the genital area, kissing and sucking around the area before moving in to play with his cock and balls. You will probably want to masturbate your partner at this stage, but watch his reactions closely, as you do not want orgasm to be reached too soon. You may now want to straddle your partner and bring his genitals into contact with yours.

Massage can be enhanced by the use of feathers, oils, lubricants, vibrators, other sex toys and even a little dirty talk, too.

When massaging, always remember to watch closely the reactions of your partner. If he flinches and looks anxious or uncomfortable at any point, try something else. If he sighs with contentment, then you can be confident that you are giving him pleasure, so continue what you are doing.

Sex toys

Tools, or sex toys, to enhance sexual pleasure, have been part of the human sexual experience since prehistoric times, although nowadays there are many more good-quality toys than ever. They are easily available from sex shops, by mail order or from Internet traders. The basic rule about sex toys is: the simpler they are, the more successful they are likely to be in providing pleasure. Elaborate machines that promise bliss hardly ever deliver.

Perhaps the most popular toy among gay men is the dildo, which may or may not vibrate. The cock ring and the butt plug are also very common.

The dildo is a phallus-shaped toy – indeed, some of them have been cast from the moulds of the penises of favourite porn stars. Made from plastic or rubber, they come in a bewildering range of shapes and sizes, and there will be something to suit all tastes. Some of them vibrate for an extra overload of sensual delight, and some have two heads so that lovers can use them simultaneously.

If you are introducing a dildo into your lovemaking, ensure that it has a handle or rope on the end so that it can be extracted easily. Always use a lubricant, and don't be too rough if you are using toys to pleasure your partner, as they can be unyielding and cause damage to the fragile anal canal.

If more than one person is going to use a dildo, ensure that it is well washed between uses – preferably with a gentle sterilizing solution (the sort of product that is used to clean babies' bottles).

Love balls are a string of small plastic or wooden spheres that are inserted into the anus, then pulled out slowly during orgasm to intensify the experience. These should be regularly cleaned in the same way as the dildo.

ABOVE Kachina dolls are religious artefacts made by the Hopi Indians of Arizona and each represents a tribal spirit. This one, from the nineteenth century, is painted with phallic symbols and probably represents fertility.

Butt plugs are solid, tapering pieces of rubber or plastic. They are intended to be pushed gently into the anus. They differ from dildos in that they are intended merely to dilate the anus, making it easier later to penetrate. Some people like to keep their butt plug in for an extended period.

Always lubricate the butt plug well before inserting it and wash it in the same way as a dildo.

When you explore the world of sex toys, you will invariably come across the sex doll, a full-size mannequin with all the right anatomical features for your pleasure. Your doll will have an accommodating mouth and anus, and probably a vibrating penis.

Some of these sex dolls are very crudely manufactured, while the more expensive models can be most luxuriously and realistically made, with recordings of dirty talk and authentic-feeling skin.

Pornography

Men are much more easily aroused by what they see than are most women. This is the reason why pornography is such an overwhelmingly male preoccupation.

Pornography and other erotic images are very popular among gay men, and they serve a useful purpose in providing sexual stimulation for those for whom a partner is unavailable, or when extra excitement is needed to spice up a masturbation session. Porno can also be an excellent educational tool, too, showing graphically the many ways that sexual expression is possible for gay men.

Most of the time the porno movie makers behave responsibly and insist on safer sex practices by their actors. Condoms are ubiquitous when anal penetration is involved, although there is little effort to eroticize the actual putting on of the rubber. Some

LEFT Erotic images of the male form have been popular throughout history. Now with the invention of photography, erotica and pornography have reached heights of sophistication and explicitness unimaginable to earlier generations.

adult movies, though, show dangerous sex practices and encourage reckless unprotected sex.

Enjoy and learn from adult movies, but ensure that if you come across deliberately dangerous scenes, or movies that were made before the advent of AIDS, when condoms were thought unnecessary, then think carefully about the consequences of imitating this behaviour.

XXX-rated movies can sometimes cause people to have unrealistic expectations about what is possible. Always remember that the actors in these films are human just like you. Their apparently incredible feats of endurance and acrobatics (and multiple orgasms) are often the product of skilful editing rather than sexual prowess. Even porno actors can lose an erection sometimes (although such moments are likely to end up on the cutting-room floor).

Bisexuality

Some people's sexuality does not take easily to being labelled as 'gay' or 'straight'; their orientation is fluid and can change with their circumstances and at different times of their life. Many men who think of themselves as gay will sometimes have a sexual adventure with a woman, and the same is true in reverse of men who consider themselves basically straight. The attraction they feel towards an individual will not always be dictated by the gender of that person, but by their personal qualities and attractiveness.

Experimentation and changing desires are a natural part of many people's sexual make-up, and although it can be bewildering for some (particularly husbands and wives who suddenly find that their spouse is in love with someone else – of the same sex), it is part of the natural order. If your sexual orientation is not as fixed as some people would like it to be, be assured that you are not abnormal, you are simply human.

Sadomasochism

S & M is a byway of sex that appeals to a large number of people, although some are so intrigued and attracted by it that they make it the focus of their entire sex life. Others simply get a thrill from the idea of submission and domination.

Even the mildest sexual activity contains some elements of restraint and coercion – slapping, biting, tickling, holding your partner down and handling him roughly will be common in most sexual encounters. Many people like to take it a stage further. Tying your partner to the bed so that he is at your mercy is a common fantasy that is easily brought to fruition by two

ABOVE Sadomasochism ranges from mild submission and domination to full-scale master–slave scenes. It often involves fetish clothing, such as leather and denim decorated with chains, and accessories such as handcuffs and whips.

consenting adults. Handcuffs and other, more elaborate, kinds of bondage gear are easily available from sex shops and on the Internet. Whether you want simply to dabble with a bit of spanking and bondage or take it much further with whips, restraints and pretend torture equipment will be up to you.

The crucial word here is consent. Although one of the participants is agreeing to give up his autonomy for the period of the encounter, there should always be a 'stop' signal that both will recognize and honour.

Needless to say, never allow yourself to be restrained, tied up or made completely vulnerable by someone you do not know and trust. Trust is an essential element in S&M.

Seasoned S&M practitioners know the rules and will be familiar with the intricacies and nuances of master–slave relationships, but for those who simply want to try it out, a basic scenario might involve one partner tying the other's hands to a headboard, maybe with silk scarves, ties or other binding material that will not cause damage. You may also want to tie his feet so that he is totally immobilized.

You can then begin to torment him with promises of sexual pleasures that are offered and then withdrawn. You can tickle him with feathers or lick his body in places that you know will drive him wild. Once you have teased him enough with these cruel, unfulfilled promises of sexual indulgence, you can move on to the real thing. All the time, however, you will be in control of what is done, and your partner will have no alternative but to allow you to use his body for your own pleasure (in the process, of course, providing enormous pleasure for him).

So long as you have agreed a code word or signal that indicates that your partner wishes to stop, you can use him in any way that takes your fancy, and he, of course, must endure the application to his body of your every whim. It is a scary and exciting experience to know that you are a helpless object for someone else's pleasure.

Mild corporal punishment could be involved, slapping the buttocks or hitting with a cane, if that is desired or thought to be exciting.

Fetishes

These are common in the gay world and usually involve particular types of clothing – leather, rubber, denim, uniforms, work gear, boots and so on. These clothes are a very strong turn-on for some people and they go to great lengths to ensure that they always play a part in their sexual adventures.

Fetishists can become obsessed with the object of their excitement, and this can become boring for partners who do not share their enthusiasm. But as part of a balanced approach to sex, fetishes can heighten excitement and fuel fantasies.

The most potent sex organ

The *Kama Sutra* encourages and lauds the explorations of sex. It calls on lovers to experiment and try almost anything that will increase the erotic charge. We have looked at only a small number of the endless ways in which gay men can pleasure each other – during the course of your erotic journey through life, you will doubtless discover many more.

The way to experience the ultimate orgasm, the climax that involves the whole body, is to employ the most powerful sexual organ of all – your imagination.

index

PICTURE CREDITS

AKG
Page 69, 75, 100, 102, 107, 113, 121
127, 131, 136, 137

Art Archive
Page 103, 117, 128

The Bridgeman Art Library
Page 81, 89, 114, 125

Christie's Images Ltd
Page 139

Werner Forman Archive
Page 112, 135